The
ITT Key Issues
Lecture Series

is made possible through a grant from
International Telephone and Telegraph Corporation

This series of lectures took place
from October 1977 to February 1978
at New York University
College of Business and Public Administration

Economic Growth or Stagnation: The Future of the U.S. Economy

Edited by

Jules Backman
New York University

With a Foreword by
Harold S. Geneen

Bobbs-Merrill Educational Publishing
Indianapolis

Copyright © 1978 by The Bobbs-Merrill Company, Inc. Printed in the
United States of America All rights reserved. No part of this book shall be
reproduced or transmitted in any form or by any means, electronic or
mechanical, including photocopying, recording, or by any information or
retrieval system, without written permission from the Publisher:

The Bobbs-Merrill Company, Inc.
4300 West 62nd Street
Indianapolis, Indiana 46268

First Edition
First Printing 1978

Library of Congress Cataloging in Publication Data

Main entry under title:

The future of the U.S. economy

(The Key issues lecture series)
1. United States—Economic policy—1971- —Addresses, essays, lectures.
I. Backman, Jules, 1910-
HC106.7.87   330.9'73'092   78-10874
ISBN-0-672-97323-5
ISBN 0-672-97322-7 pbk.

Contents

Contents

Tables

Preface

Abraham L. Gitlow

Dean, New York University
College of Business and Public Administration

The Key Issues Lecture Series at the College of Business and Public Administration, New York University, is now represented by seven volumes of these important lectures. This volume, the seventh in the series, is a collection of the papers presented under the general topic, "Economic Growth or Stagnation : The Future of the United States' Economy." The topic was selected because of deep and growing concern over a variety of shocks which have been buffeting the American economy, such as a huge U.S. trade deficit, a continuing decline in the value of the dollar in international currency markets, a steady increase in protectionism, continuing concern over energy policy and raw material availability, as well as concern over the adequacy of investment and the rate of advance in technology. Could these concerns be interpreted to mean that the American economic giant is entering a period of reduced economic growth or stagnation with continuing high levels of unemployment? What will be the consequences of our efforts to develop an energy policy and to improve the environment? It is our hope that the papers included in this volume will provide insight and intelligent understanding in connection with these most serious questions.

The Key Issues Lecture Series has been made possible by a grant from the International Telephone and Telegraph Corporation. Its organizer is Professor Jules Backman, to whom all credit for the series is due. To both ITT and Professor Backman go the College's deep appreciation, for the series has enabled the College to enhance its role in advancing public understanding of many major contemporary issues.

The lecturers whose papers are included in this volume are a distinguished group, and we are completely confident that this volume will receive the excellent reception its predecessors have enjoyed.

My personal appreciation goes also to Catherine Ferfoglia, Professor Backman's secretary and principal aide in preparing the volume for publication, and to my administrative assistants, Susan Greenbaum and Virginia Moress.

Foreword

Harold S. Geneen
Chairman of the Board
International Telephone and Telegraph Corporation

I think the 1970s will be remembered as the decade when the American business community, the American government, and the American people woke up to the fact that the United States no longer is the sole industrial giant of the world.

The great influx of foreign products signal a phenomenon Americans can no longer ignore: the domestic marketplace can no longer be considered the private domain of American business. Just as multinational corporations such as ITT have developed foreign marketplaces for our products so, too, have foreign corporations aimed their products at our shores.

This "reverse flow" has brought the world closer today to becoming a single market than it has been at any time in history. But this exchange has complicated the job of economic forecasters and futurologists who must interpret the rise and decline in levels of economic activity.

With so many external factors now added to our economic equation, orthodox explanations of peaks and troughs—using the changing tides of replenishing or expanding stocks of durable capital goods as indicators—no longer will bring the expected results.

This Key Issues Lecture Series at NYU on the prospects for economic growth versus stagnation was designed to find new yardsticks of economic measurement and to assess our growth potential for the immediate future.

Dr. Jules Backman, who moderated the series, has brought together an excellent group of nationally known business thought leaders. This volume should help clarify the policy issues facing a world that has moved a long way toward economic unity and should serve as a timely contribution to the literature of economic change.

ONE

Economic Growth or Stagnation:

An Overview

Jules Backman
Research Professor Emeritus of Economics
New York University

The persistence of large-scale unemployment in the 1970s has once again raised the spectre of a mature economy. Some observers are proclaiming that we face a new period of economic stagnation, that the sharp gains in economic activity during the past three decades will not be repeated, and that we face a future characterized by continuing high-level unemployment and price inflation.*

The causes of this deep pessimism are claimed to be demographic, social, and economic. Population is growing at the slowest rate in our history. It is estimated that raw materials are becoming scarcer and that this will place a significant constraint upon economic growth. It is noted that energy costs have skyrocketed because of the oil cartel and that we face shortages in this area. It is feared that available supplies of capital will not be adequate to support the required rates of economic growth. It is believed that new technological breakthroughs will be less dramatic than in the past few decades. We are being choked by a polluted environment. The shift to a service economy will act as a drag on economic growth because of slower productivity gains in this sector.

*My special thanks to Marvin Levine who provided valuable assistance in the collection of materials.

1

These forces are aggravated by a number of other factors. The work ethic has been weakened in recent decades in a society in which a wide range of progams, such as welfare, food stamps, medicare, medicaid, unemployment compensation, has been developed to protect individuals and families against economic hardships. Our permissive society has been accompanied by a disintegration of the family, the development of a drug culture, and by a marked lowering of moral and ethical standards. Major cities are in serious difficulties. Widespread disillusionment has developed with government and with the institutional arrangements in our society. Minority groups make progress too slowly.

One additional factor must be underlined. Much of the recent pessimism concerning long-term growth prospects developed during the 1973-75 recession and was no doubt influenced by the fact that it was our largest post-World War II recession. It is not clear to what extent cyclical trends have been confused with secular or long-term trends. We do know that during periods of declining economic activity, for example, productivity tends to lag but then catches up during recovery. It is not clear to what extent demographic trends—later marriages, delayed births, reductions in family size—were affected.

This list of perceived problem areas could be extended. But it is essentially an emphasis upon the negative. Is there no hope?

Such a chorus of pessimism is not new—only the identified ills change. In the early days of the industrial revolution, it was the slums, the bad working conditions in the factories, poor medical care, the exploitation of children, the poverty of the masses—a condition which still exists in many parts of the world—et cetera.

In the 1930s, it was claimed that our secular growth trend had leveled off and that we had entered a period of economic maturity. The era of rapid growth and economic expansion was over; downturns would become longer and deeper, while upswings would be shorter and less pronounced. Outlets for investable funds would be much less than in the past; thus, we would have to learn to save less and to consume more. It was asserted that population growth was slowing down, the frontiers had all been opened, and no new technological breakthroughs were probable.

The period following World War II was supposed to be accompanied by mass unemployment in the U.S., major countries would be so overcome by wartime devastation that recovery would be prevented for decades (the dramatic recoveries of defeated Germany and Japan were not foreseen), large-scale depressions would again develop, the volume of world trade would remain low and so on.

Yes, we have always had our Jeremiahs. But despite their woeful forecasts, marked economic and social progress has been characteristic of this country and other leading nations. Somehow, "we have overcome." And we shall do so again.

Despite the current pessimism, we stand at all-time peaks as measured by numerous economic indicators including total employment, real gross national product, real per capita income, and average levels of living.

We are making considerable progress in reducing pollution, in curtailing job discrimination, in creating equal educational opportunities, and in improving health care. We are gradually overcoming the national trauma created by the Vietnam War and Watergate.

We continue to maintain economic and political freedom. In the various proposals for deregulation, such as those for airlines and natural gas, there is a growing recognition that economic freedom is more effective than government regulation in achieving the goal of the better life.

Clearly, the fact that economic growth continues demonstrates that there are powerful forces for growth which have been overcoming the perceived effects of the problem areas. Nevertheless, the areas emphasized by the pessimists do reflect problems which have emerged into the public consciousness in the past few years. The critical questions are: how do we contend with these problems and how do we place them in proper perspective? There is wide disagreement concerning the outlook for long-term economic growth: the spectrum of opinion ranges from the exceedingly optimistic to the exceedingly pessimistic. As will be developed later, it appears probable that between now and the end of this century—although the rate of economic growth will be somewhat lower than the high levels of the 1960s—our economy will still be marked by further significant advances in the real level of living.

DEFINITION OF TERMS

Various meanings have been associated with the term *stagnation.* In the 1930s, Professor Alvin Hansen, a leading exponent of the secular stagnation thesis, pointed out that it represented "sick recoveries which die in their infancy and depressions which feed on themselves and leave a hard and seemingly immovable core of unemployment."[1] It was basically a no-growth economy!

However, in more recent years, stagnation has been given a significantly different meaning. The current stagnationists believe that our economy is not growing rapidly enough to absorb the increase in the labor force. Thus, emphasis has shifted from a no-growth economy to one in which the rate of growth is not sufficiently strong to provide a sufficient number of jobs for those able and and willing to work.

How is economic stagnation to be measured—in *total* real Gross National Product (GNP) or in *per capita* real income? In terms of economic welfare of the individual, the significant measure is total real income per capita. Increases in that total can be translated substantially into ever higher levels of living, the extent of the increase depending in part on the changes in the burden of taxation.

On the other hand, in terms of resources available to finance various activities of government—such as defense, social welfare, et cetera—or in measuring employment opportunities, total real GNP would be the more meaningful concept. We must recognize that part of both total real GNP and per capita real income are now being utilized to improve the quality of life so that increases do not translate automatically into comparable gains in levels of living. However, the increases can be translated into total well-being (level of living plus improvements in the quality of living).[2]

What do we mean by economic growth? Any increase from its current level or a rise in line with past experience? Or a rate of advance large enough to yield high levels of economic activity and relatively low levels of idle resources, particularly unemployment?

The distinction is important because recent population trends and all projections of population indicate a much slower rate of increase in the last quarter of the twentieth century than in the preceding twenty-five years. This factor alone could reduce the rate of increase in *total* real GNP by at least 0.5 percentage points in the years ahead.

In this analysis, we will consider stagnation to mean little or no growth in total real GNP or in total real income per capita. Increases in these measures represent economic growth. This still leaves the question of whether or not the rate of increase is adequate to permit the required growth in employment opportunities.

Before analyzing the alleged causes cited by the new stagnationists, it is useful to review briefly the stagnation theories advanced during the 1930s and how they were disproved during the post-World War II period.

THE MATURE ECONOMY THESIS OF THE THIRTIES

During the severe depression of the 1930s, some economists questioned the ability of the American economy to grow. It was suggested that our economy had reached a mature state for several reasons: (1) the rate of population growth was declining; (2) territorial expansion had come to an end; (3) future technological advances would be limited; and (4) as a result of the first three developments, there would be a shortage of investment opportunities.

The stagnationists argued that the increase in population had been a major factor responsible for much of the capital formation in the nineteenth century. They believed that in some countries the rate of population growth was close to zero. It was their contention that this significant change in population trends removed one of the important dynamic and autonomous inducements to invest in the Western world.[3]

They ignored the fact that the *rate of population growth* actually had been declining in the United States since 1850. Table 1.1 shows the population trends by decades from 1850 to 1940. The rate of population increase fell from 35.6 percent in the decade from 1850 to 1860 to 26.6 percent from 1860 to 1870 and recorded only minor changes in the next two decades. In the first decade of the twentieth century, the rate of increase averaged about 21 percent and then fell below 15 percent in the 1910-20 period. In the booming decade of the 1920s, the increase of 16.1 percent was only slightly above that of the prior decade. In the decade from 1930 to 1940, the rate of increase fell to 7.2 percent. As has been pointed out " . . . the rate of population growth began to decline in the latter half of the nineteenth century and that therefore this cannot serve as one of the secular causes of the Great Depression . . . ."[4]

According to Professor Alvin Hansen, the closing of the frontier

Table 1.1   Changes in Population, By Decades, 1850-1940

	Number	Increase	%
1850	23,191,876		
1860	31,443,321	8,251,445	35.6
1870	39,818,449	8,375,128	26.6
1880	50,155,783	10,337,334	26.0
1890	62,947,714	12,791,931	25.5
1900	75,994,575	13,046,861	20.7
1910	91,972,266	15,977,691	21.0
1920	105,710,620	13,738,354	14.9
1930	122,775,046	17,064,426	16.1
1940	131,669,275	8,894,229	7.2

SOURCE: U.S. Department of Commerce, *Statistical Abstract of the United States, 1971* (Washington, D.C.: U.S. Bureau of the Census, 1971), p. 5.

meant that "these outlets for new investment are rapidly being closed."[5] He concluded that not only had the settlement of the West been completed but also there were reduced opportunities for foreign investment. The stagnationists argued that, although opportunity existed for foreign investment in the backward areas of the world, there was little reason to believe that these areas could experience the development as well as the growth of new territory that was experienced in the nineteenth century. This rationale ignored the fact that the frontier in the U.S. had disappeared toward the close of the nineteenth century.[6]

The fundamental error in the emphasis upon the disappearing frontier was the assumption that economic growth depended in large measure on an *extensive* use of land — the opening up of new territories. It ignored the enormous expansion that could be achieved through an *intensive* use of land and other resources such as has been realized in recent decades; this is discussed at a later point.

The third element in the mature economy thesis related to technological progress. Professor Hansen believed that "population growth and the penetration into new territories . . . played an important role in the widening of the market and the development of mass production techniques. Extensive expansion minimized the risks of technological innovations and encouraged bold experimentation."[7] Such areas as railroads, electric power, and automobiles had created tremendous investment opportunities. The stagnationists believed that there were no new major technological developments which could provide a similar stimulus for growth.

But such forebodings were not new. Thus, in his *First Annual Report*, Colonel Carroll D. Wright, U.S. Commissioner of Labor, expressed concern about the destabilizing effects of "speculative railroad building." He indicated that because of the crucial economic importance of this area, this situation did not bode well for the economy.[8]

The outlook for new technological developments was believed to be dismal because many institutional forces were adversely affecting initiative and opportunity. These forces included the increased power of trade unions, concentration of monopoly power, and the emphasis upon nonprice competition.

Despite these forebodings, during the past third of a century, there has been a technological explosion which has contributed significantly to the enormous economic growth we have experienced since the 1930s.

DEVELOPMENTS AFTER WORLD WAR II

The deep pessimism of the stagnationists during the 1930s was proved to be completely unfounded by the experience in the post-World War II period when we enjoyed significant economic growth.

Between 1929 and 1939, real gross national product recorded little net increase. Then during World War II, the total increased from $320 billion (in 1972 dollars) in 1939 to $559 billion in 1945. With minor interruptions, the expansion continued throughout the postwar years; the total exceeded $1,300 billion in 1977.

The fears of the 1930s concerning population growth, technology, and new investment opportunities were not realized as is shown below.

Population Growth

Following World War II there was a marked increase in the birth rate due to the vastly improved economic conditions and to catch up for the low level in the 1930s.[9] The birth rate increased from 18.7 per 1000 of the population to 20.4 in 1945, 24.1 in 1950, and reached a high of 25.3 in 1957. Since that date it has declined significantly until in 1976 it was around 15, placing it at a significantly lower level than in the depression years of the mid-1930s.[10] A small increase developed in 1977 with some experts projecting a further rise from the low 1976 level.[11]

According to the U.S. Bureau of the Census, the median age of first marriages in 1930 was 24.3 for males and 21.3 for the females; in 1955, it was 22.6 for males and 20.2 for females.[12] It has been pointed out that "Before World War II, about 53 percent of all women between twenty and twenty-four were married; by 1955, the proportion was 71 percent and has remained there."[13]

Young married couples were endeavoring to catch up for lost time and the birth rate was favorably influenced. Since the late 1950s, the concept of the "proper" size of the family has been revised downward again partly because of a desire on the part of many young couples to upgrade their level of living. The increasing importance of the Women's Liberation movement and the greater desire for a more "professionally" oriented life reduced the emphasis on home life. The increased use of the pill and other contraceptive devices and the increasing use of abortion also contributed to the lower birth rate.

Research and Development Trends

After the end of World War II, there was a tremendous burst of technology with the accompanying development of new industries and new products. In part, this reflected wartime developments and, later, it represented a spinoff from our large expenditures for space research. It also reflected an increased understanding of the yields to be derived from large-scale research and development (R & D) and hence the interest by many companies in this type of investment. (See Table 1.2.)

R & D expenditures in current dollars almost doubled from 1945 to 1950 and again from 1950 to 1955 and more than doubled in the next five years. Since 1960, the rate of increase has been substantially lower than in the earlier post-World War II period. Nevertheless, the increases have been significant.[14]

Although price inflation has added significantly to the costs of R &

Table 1.2   Research and Development Expenditures, Selected Years, 1945-76

	Total [billions]	% Increase In 5 Years	% of Gross National Product
1945	$ 1.8	—	0.85%
1950	3.4	88.9%	1.19
1955	6.2	83.0	1.55
1960	13.6	120.0	2.69
1965	20.1	47.8	2.92
1970	26.0	30.0	2.85
1975	35.2	35.4	2.32
1976	38.1	—	2.25

SOURCES: National Science Foundation; McGraw-Hill, Department of Economics; and U.S. Department of Commerce, Bureau of Economic Analysis.

D, as it has to all sectors of the economy, even after allowing for this factor, there has been a significant expansion over the past 30 years.

Government spending on R & D increased during most of the post-World War II period. It amounted to about 65 percent of the total in the 1960s and now accounts for close to 53 percent.[15] The development of atomic energy and space explorations yielded many new products for civilian use.

In the private sector, such areas as chemicals, drugs, textiles, computers, and electronics have developed a multitude of new products. In the drug field, for example, many new ethical drugs were developed after intensive research and development. However, the flow of new drug products has slowed up significantly as the Food and Drug Administration has tightened up its regulations.

The sharp rise in R & D made a significant contribution to economic growth in the past three decades. The many new products that have poured forth from the research laboratories have provided a leavening influence on economic growth. This trend is likely to continue in the foreseeable future.

Intensive Use of Resources

As a society, we have continuously developed a more efficient use of resources. This can best be illustrated by developments in agriculture where a literal explosion in terms of output per farm worker has developed over the past half century. Thus, using the year 1967 as equal to 100, it rose from 17 in 1929 to 33 in 1947 and 136 in 1975. From 1929 to 1947, output per farm worker almost doubled and then increased by over 300 percent from 1947 to 1975.[16] American farmers have invested substantial sums in modern capital equipment and have significantly increased output per worker and per acre. Today, investment per worker in farming is more than double that in manufacturing. Modern technology has been spectacular on the farm. New fertilizers, hybrid seeds, and plant disease control have revolutionized food production. The farmer has learned how to make much better use of existing agricultural resources.

There are many other illustrations of the more intensive use of resources ranging from thin tinplate which made possible the production of more tin cans per ton to the reduction in the amount of coal required to produce one kilowatt hour of electricity, to the various developments in the electronics industry with the introduction first of the transistor and later of miniaturization.

Growth In Investment

The shortage of investment opportunities anticipated by the stagnationists disappeared after World War II as a result of the developments described earlier. Table 1.3 shows the growth in total fixed investment in real dollars before and after World War II.

That enormous investment opportunities developed is evident from these data. The total real investment in 1976 was five times as large as in 1939 or in 1945.

The above analysis has clearly demonstrated that each of the four assumptions underlying the stagnationist theory of the 1930s has turned out to be completely wrong. This doesn't necessarily mean that the theories being advanced by the new stagnationists automatically should be ignored. But it does indicate the importance of examining them separately and in combination to determine whether or not they provide a sound enough rationale to reverse a growth trend which has persisted, with some interruptions, for some 200 years.

Table 1.3   Total Fixed Investment in 1972 Dollars, Selected Years, 1929-77

	Total [billions]	Nonresidential [billions]
1929	$ 51.3	$ 37.0
1939	32.0	20.7
1945	31.4	27.6
1950	83.2	50.0
1955	96.3	61.2
1960	101.0	66.0
1965	138.8	95.6
1970	150.4	110.0
1973	190.7	131.0
1975	151.5	112.7
1977	184.0	127.1

SOURCE: *Economic Report of the President* (Washington: Council of Economic Advisers, January 1978), p. 258.

THE PROBLEM AREAS

As was noted earlier, the new stagnationists have been emphasizing several areas of concern: lower population growth, higher energy prices, environmental costs, raw materials availability, capital shortages, and the continuing shift to a service economy.

Slower Growth In Population and Labor Force

The annual rate of total economic growth will be lower in the balance of the twentieth century than in the past three decades because population will be growing at a slower rate. The realization of this projection for population would reduce the annual growth rate for real GNP by about 0.5 percentage points.[17]

These demographic trends will hold down the rate of increase in total demand for goods and services. The stimulating impact on total demand of a rapidly rising population will be smaller than in the past thirty years. This tendency will be reinforced by the steadily larger proportion of total population which is over 65 years of age—from 8.0 percent in 1950 to 10.5 percent in 1975, and a projected 12 percent in

2000, and 17 percent in 2025.[18] Senior citizens tend to reduce their total demand for goods and services as their incomes decline and to change the composition of that demand; for example, medical care increases in importance while purchases of household goods decline.

The slower rate of growth in total population also will result in a lower growth rate for the total labor force. The U.S. Bureau of Labor Statistics has projected that "the labor force should grow at an annual rate of 1.9 percent in the latter half of the 1970s, and only 1.1 percent a year during the 1980s, compared with a rate of increase of 2.3 percent during the first half of the 1970s."[19]

Total employment can increase somewhat more rapidly than population for two reasons:

1. The participation of women in the labor market has been rising rapidly. In 1956, 36 percent of all women who were aged 20 and over were in the labor force. By 1976, the proportion had risen to 47 percent. This increase has been attributed by the Council of Economic Advisers to the following factors: " . . . increased potential earnings in the labor market; later marriages; a decline in birth rates; more efficient production in the home because of such time-saving consumer durables as freezers and dishwashers; and a change in attitudes concerning the roles of men and women."[20]

A further increase in the participation rate of women is probable in the years ahead.

2. A reversal of the trend toward earlier retirements would add to the labor force. To a significant degree, the purchasing power of senior citizens is dependent upon social security payments. These payments are tied to changes in the consumer price index *(CPI)* and have been increasing rapidly in recent years in response to inflationary pressures. Nevertheless, social security payments represent a significant decline in income for recipients in relation to their earnings when employed.

Stripped of all the technical jargon, those who are retired must be supported by those who are working. Under present policies, the number of retirees will represent an increasing proportion of the total population. This trend necessitates a reevaluation of and change in our compulsory retirement policy. As a result of the expected increase in the life span of men and women, by the year 2000 more workers will not only be mandatorily retired but also will have a larger number of years of retirement.

The retirement age of sixty-five years reflected largely the mass unemployment of the 1930s and was designed to provide jobs for younger workers. Many workers who are now retired at sixty-five years or younger are able and desirous of continuing in the labor force. In many cases, they have valuable skills that could be of immeasurable benefit to society.

To reduce the social security burden and to meet the labor needs of an expanding economy, many of these senior citizens should be continued in the labor force. There is already evidence that this problem is being recognized. In April 1978, a new law raised the mandatory retirement age to seventy years in the private sector. However, college teachers with full tenure are not affected until July 1, 1982 and corporate executives with annual retirement benefits of $27,000 or more can be retired at 65 years.[21]

Victor Fuchs projects that employment will "grow almost as rapidly" through 1990 as in the past fifteen years but the growth rate will "decelerate markedly" after 1990. On balance, the size of the labor force should increase more slowly in the decades ahead with the accompanying smaller rate of increase in total GNP.

Higher Energy Prices

Cheap and abundant energy has played a key role in America's past economic growth. However, the era of cheap energy is over. The almost four-fold increase in crude oil prices in recent years has been accompanied by a major rise in the costs of all types of energy. This dramatic change will affect the allocation of resources, the structure of industry, the types of energy developed and used, the location of industry (e.g. development of reliable solar energy is more probable in the sunbelt than in the industrial midwest and northeast), and the rate of economic growth.

It has been estimated that a slower growth in the supply of energy will shave only a small fraction off the growth rate [e.g. 0.1 or 0.2 percent]. This estimate may be statistically correct if we consider only the relative importance of energy per se as a component of real GNP. But the qualitative impact on industrial processes, the relative attractiveness of the use of capital as compared with labor, or among uses of capital for higher-cost energy are the real problems. Certainly cost-benefit calculations will continue to be significantly affected by this marked increase in the relative price of energy.

Professor Dale Jorgenson of Harvard has pointed out that the higher cost of energy has lowered the energy intensity of production as well as the capital intensity and as a result "the new combination of labor, capital, energy and materials is less productive than it was before OPEC emerged."[22] Some of the existing capital stock acquired at a time when energy was much lower in cost has now become obsolete and projects that were attractive at the far lower level of energy prices no longer are viable. Thus, as Jorgenson suggests the "average job in the economy will be less capital-intensive and therefore less productive."

The significantly higher oil prices have increased costs and reduced efficiency by necessitating the development of new, higher-priced energy and methods of production. It also has created pressures to use energy more efficiently. Savings in energy of between 15 and 20 percent of output in the next five years in the industrial sector have been forecast.

Higher costs for energy and possible shortages will affect rates of growth in the industrial economies throughout the world. Even the Soviet Union is not immune to these pressures. A Central Intelligence Agency report forecasts a lower rate of economic growth in Russia in the 1980s since "the most serious problem is a looming oil shortage."[23]

However, it must be emphasized that "the basic problem of energy is its cost, not an absolute limit on availability."[24] The solution for the energy shortage, therefore, is not found in conservation measures alone. Major emphasis must be given to policies which would lead to an expansion of output.

Historically, proven supplies of petroleum continually have been grossly underestimated as the following summary indicates:

> . . . the doomsayers have not only been consistently vocal, they have also been consistently wrong. America has had less than a dozen years' supply of oil left for a hundred years. In 1866 the United States Revenue Commission was concerned about having synthetics available when crude oil production ended; in 1891 the U.S. Geological Survey assured us there was little chance of oil in Texas; and in 1914 the Bureau of Mines estimated total future U.S. production at 6 billion barrels—we have

produced that much oil every twenty months for years. Perhaps the most curious thing about these forecasts is a tendency for remaining resources to grow as we deplete existing resources. Thus, a geologist for the world's largest oil company estimated potential U.S. reserves at 110 billion to 165 billion barrels in 1948. In 1959, after we had consumed almost 30 billion of those barrels, he estimated 391 billion were left.[25]

We do not know how much additional supplies of petroleum and natural gas will be forthcoming at higher prices nor what conservation measures would be adopted. But that domestic supplies would be larger and effective demand would be smaller is the lesson of experience. The net result would be to reduce our dependence on OPEC with an accompanying favorable effect upon our international balance of payments. These results can best be achieved through the unhampered operation of the price system. New forms of energy and economies in the uses of existing forms can play a significant part if we permit market forces to perform their vital role.

We have come to the end of an era in which expanding supplies of low-cost natural gas and petroleum have dominated the energy markets. Now, we must turn to other sources of energy which are available—in some instances in unlimited amounts—but at higher prices. Solar energy, geothermal energy,[26] coal, oil shale, nuclear power, and small hydroelectric plants are some of the sources which can be developed. Even windmills and trash[27] can be used to generate energy.

The combination of research and development, higher prices, and tax incentives can help to meet all of our demands for energy and enable us to reduce significantly our present dependence on the OPEC countries for almost half our petroleum needs. The major thrust of national policy must be to expand supplies with conservation measures as a supplementary factor. Emphasis primarily on conservation measures will act to retard economic growth.

It is important we recognize that prices have a rationing function as well as a stimulating function. The concern in some quarters that profits will increase sharply if natural gas prices are raised indicates concern only with the stimulating function. Ignored is the role of higher prices in compelling a more efficient use of energy by eliminating or reducing less essential demands for natural gas. This latter role is of great importance if a new balance is to be brought between supply and demand for natural gas as well as for other forms of energy.

Government interference with the operation of the price system not only results in a less efficient allocation of resources but also is accompanied by a considerable burden of administrative costs. Professor Paul MacAvoy has reported that:

> On the basis of an investigation and analysis stretching over the last half of 1976, the Task Force on Reform of Federal Energy Administration Regulation concluded that FEA regulation imposed significant costs on markets for refined products. The petroleum industry paid reporting and administrative compliance costs approaching $500 million annually, and firms were subject to extensive governmental interference with the conduct of normal business activities. In addition, taxpayers paid $47 million or more each year to maintain FEA's regulatory program.[28]

These costs must be recovered from consumers in the form of higher prices or result in lower profits.

Although higher energy charges should have some negative impact on economic growth, it is not inevitable that the result will be so adverse that it will lead to economic stagnation—particularly if public policy emphasizes the expansion of alternative sources of energy.

Environment and Economic Growth

Antipollution laws require business to spend billions of dollars to develop a cleaner environment. Programs to improve the environment affect growth rates by diverting capital from plant and equipment expansion.[29]

Expenditures for new plant and equipment for pollution abatement amounted to $6.8 billion in 1976 and was expected to rise to $7.5 billion in 1977.[30] Although spending on pollution abatement was only slightly above 5 percent of total plant and equipment expenditures, in some broadly defined industries, such as nonferrous metals (19 percent), paper (15 percent), steel (15 percent), and chemicals (11 percent), the proportion was much higher. For parts of these industries, the relative importance of such spending is much greater as Norma Pace points out in Chapter 3.

To the extent these types of investment replace expansion in plant and equipment, the rate of growth in gross national product is being adversely affected. Edward F.Denison has estimated that in 1975, output per unit of input was reduced by 0.5 percentage point because of pollution controls, measures to protect safety and health, and the rise in dishonesty and crime; 0.23 percentage point was accounted for by pollution control.[31] A sound policy would be to enforce a reduction in pollution through tax incentives while encouraging the overall economic growth that will allow us to pay for the improved quality of life without reducing the level of living. As Norma Pace points out, " . . . capital formation is a necessary part of solving environmental and social problems."

What will be the total spending for pollution abatement in future years? The estimates vary widely. According to Dr. Lewis J. Perl of National Economic Research Associates, "By 1983 between 3% and 6% of GNP and between 7% and 10% of total gross private domestic investment would be expended to comply with federal clean air and water legislation."[32]

A lower cost has been projected in a study by the Congressional Joint Economic Committee: " . . . the ratio of annual environmental improvement costs . . . rises from 1 percent of the GNP to 3 percent in the year 2000. This is not a large portion of our increase in income. We give up only a tenth of one percentage point in annual growth of national output to pay for the active abatement policy."[33]

Even if this estimate proves to be too modest, it suggests that the real cost of reducing pollution is relatively smaller than is generally believed. Moreover, the somewhat smaller increase in the level of living will be offset by an improved quality of life. On balance, we will have a higher level of economic well-being but the mix will include a greater quality of life component.[34] However, it is virtually impossible to quantify the improvement in air quality, cleaner water, and less noxious odors in terms of economic well-being.

Against this background, it is clear that we should not accept the recommendations of those who have concluded that one solution for the pollution problem is to slow down or eliminate growth. There is no inseparable link between increased pollution and economic growth.

As Professor Lester C. Thurow has pointed out: "Pollution occurs because pollution is a privately costless but socially costly method of disposing of unwanted by-products."[35] The way to stop pollution is to make it expensive instead of costless. When beer bottles carried a deposit they were returned; it was costly to throw them away. When the nonreturnable bottle and can were developed, they were used to litter the environment.[36] When it is costless to dump industrial waste into the streams, it is dumped. But place a penalty [tax] upon this practice and new methods of use and disposal will be developed. Basically, to provide for the best allocation of resources, antipollution costs should include both private as well as social costs.

The added cost of handling the disposal of waste will result in some changes in the patterns of production, and the investment in pollution control equipment will reduce the capital available to finance new expansion in capacity. However, continued economic growth will make it possible to finance more easily the cost of reducing or eliminating pollution. The net cost will be a somewhat slower rate of economic growth but an offsetting increase in economic well-being. Thus, we will have allocated our productive resources in such a manner as to maximize our satisfaction.

Shortages of Raw Materials

During the strong business expansion which ended in 1973, widespread shortages of raw materials developed in this country.[37] The U.S. Department of Commerce reported that "Practical capacity ceilings were approached in some . . . industries . . . especially key materials producers, and this limited the scope for continued rapid output growth."[38] In part, the shortages reflected the failure of basic industries to expand capacity adequately in prior years because of their unfavorable profit experience. The OPEC oil boycott towards the end of 1973 combined with the subsequent efforts by other third-world countries to raise the prices of their raw materials created additional concern about potential shortages.

These developments took place shortly after the Club of Rome report had estimated that we were using up our material resources and would exhaust the world's natural resources and that in the years ahead economic growth would be constrained. Its conclusion, which created widespread concern, was, "We can thus say with some confidence that, under the assumption of no major change in the present system, population and industrial growth will certainly stop within the next century, at the latest."[39]

As a result of many critical analyses,[40] the Club of Rome subsequently modified its unduly pessimistic conclusions,[41] but the concern over potential shortages of raw materials remains.

All students of this problem are not pessimistic. The potential supply of mineral raw materials is virtually unlimited, according to Dr. Bruce Netschert in Chapter 4. Potential sources of supply include:

1. Materials in the earth's crust;
2. Ordinary igneous rocks which have "inexhaustible quantities" of metals including aluminum, iron ore, titanium, chromium, nitrates, et cetera;
3. Nodules on the sea bottom which include phosphates, magnesium, copper, nitrates, et cetera;
4. Sea water, particularly for magnesium;
5. Scrap materials for many metals;
6. Technology which makes possible more efficient use, substitution, and synthesis.

Similarly, Professor Solomon Fabricant has concluded:

. . . What we now count as resources are but a tiny fraction of the mass of our earth. In fact, resources, as defined in a valid economic sense, and the economic yield from resources, have also been increasing, and also at a geometric, not an arithmetic, rate. And it is a rate that exceeds the rate of growth of population.

I see no good reason to fear a decline in the foreseeable future in the rate of growth of resources, and of the income or output they yield, to a level below or even only down to the rate of population growth . . . [42]

It must be recognized, of course, that there may be many problems to overcome before potential supplies can be converted into actual supplies. Of particular importance would be relative price levels and technology.

The third-world countries have been a major source of raw materials for the industrial world—usually on terms of trade more favorable to the latter group of nations. The burden of widely fluctuating raw material prices has been borne largely by the producers rather than by consumers. Stimulated by the example of the oil producers, other countries have been insisting upon higher prices for their raw materials and upon a greater control over supplies. They have exerted pressure on the wealthier countries through international organizations to guarantee markets for their products at higher prices.

They also have been eager to diversify their economies by building up their manufacturing capabilities, ranging from the processing of their raw materials to the production of consumer goods. To the extent that these goals are achieved, the ability of major industrial countries to continue past growth rates may be adversely affected. Costs will rise and patterns of production used in the past will have to be changed. Substitute products will have to be developed—possibly impairing overall economic efficiency.

But the impacts need not be all adverse. Price rises act to stimulate new output and to compel a more efficient use of available supplies. Moreover, history is replete with the replacement by new and often better materials for older ones as new technology has developed, as Netschert points out in Chapter 4. Many important illustrations come readily to mind: the substitution of synthetic fibers for natural fibers, of synthetic nitrates for nitrates, the replacing of coal by petroleum and natural gas—now in the process of being reversed—and the development of new chemicals.

The frontiers of science are wide open. We are still in the very early stages of determining what raw materials can be recovered from the oceans.[43] The supply of available raw materials also is affected by price relationships and improving technology.[44] Norma Pace notes that "Technology is lowering the cost of recycling many materials and has led to the birth of a new industry—resource recovery." At higher prices oil shale would become an economically viable source of petroleum just as hard, low grade taconite developed into an important source of iron ore as a result of new technology.[45]

As the National Academy of Sciences has pointed out: "The 'doomsters' see a future in which catastrophic exhaustion of resources is inevitable unless drastic measures are taken to reduce economic growth . . . . Their gloomy outlook is based on a 'fixed' supply of materials and fails to recognize that the supply available changes as prices rise and technical advances make lower grade resources economically and physically more accessible."[46]Dr. Bruce Netschert concludes: "I find it difficult to conceive of a true scarcity situation developing in any non-fuel mineral during the coming decades, if ever . . . . the availability of mineral raw materials will not impose on the continued economic growth of the United States . . . and, for that matter, the world as a whole—for the indefinite future, if ever."

Shortages are not absolute. They reflect cost-price relationships and the stage of technology. The concept of shortage must be viewed in dynamic rather than in static terms. Our past experience suggests that given an appropriate economic environment, adequate supplies of raw materials will be available at a cost to meet the needs of an expanding economy. And that could take new forms and be derived from sources which are not now given much attention.

Capital Shortages

Capital formation plays a critical role in economic growth. Economic growth is largely dependent upon our willingness to forego current consumption (savings) and to use the resources saved to add to the supply of capital goods (investment). However, as Norma Pace spells out in Chapter 3, "The current lag in capital spending gives recognition to the possibility that the structure of the industrial world's economies may be changing and this creates doubt about the need for physical additions to the capital stock."

One possible constraint on future economic growth is a projected shortage of the supply of capital. Two aspects of projected capital shortage have been emphasized: (1) the total available savings will not be large enough, and (2) part of these savings must be diverted to improvements in environmental quality thus reducing the total available to finance economic growth.

It is an interesting commentary that fear of stagnation in the 1930s was based in part on an anticipated inadequacy of investment opportunities despite the availability of savings while in the 1980s stagnation is anticipated by some analysts because the supply of capital may not be large enough to meet the enlarged investment opportunities.

Tremendous amounts of capital investment will be required to modernize our industrial plants as well as to finance the expansion in capacity that is so urgently needed to maintain economic growth in the future. The average amount of capital invested per worker in American industry is about $40,000 with much higher investments required for chemicals and petroleum. A study by the New York Stock Exchange indicated "that the present estimated *saving* potential in the U.S. economy through 1985—from all domestic sources—is something over $4 trillion . . . . Over the same period, capital *demands* are likely to reach a cumulative total of $4.7 trillion. That leaves *an estimated capital gap of $650 billion.*"[47]

The U.S. Department of Commerce studied the capital required to reach a real level of output in line with full employment in 1980. Based on that study, the Council of Economic Advisors reported that:

> Because the ratio of business fixed investment to GNP in 1971-74 continued at the 10.4 percent level that prevailed from 1965-70, the business fixed investment to GNP ratio may have to average 12 percent from 1975 to 1980 to meet the capital requirements projected for 1980. Since investment is expected to amount to less than 10 percent of GNP in 1975-76, these estimates suggest that investment ratios even higher than 12 percent may be necessary in the next 4 years to put enough capital in place by the end of 1980 to meet the goals previously stipulated.[48]

Norma Pace estimates that this country will have to "allocate at least one percent more of its gross national product to business investment" in the next decade. To achieve this goal will require "a reduction in taxes." A more optimistic view is to be found in a Brookings study of capital needs which concluded that "the estimates indicate that with normal growth and without universal sacrifices the economy will be able to meet the capital demands that can reasonably be projected for the remainder of the decade."[49]

It must be recognized that the individual's incentive to save is being undermined by the ongoing price inflation. Returns for many types of savings have been lower than the rate of price inflation in recent years. The unattractiveness of saving is increased because income on savings is subject to taxes. The continuing erosion in the purchasing power of the dollar places a premium on current spending rather than on saving.

Corporate undistributed profits, another major source of savings, also are adversely affected by price inflation because they must be used in part to offset inflation rather than to finance economic growth. A continuation of these trends could act to erode an important underpinning of economic growth.

To obtain the enormous amount of savings needed requires an economic and tax environment conducive to saving and the availability of incentives to encourage its investment. In recent years, the reluctance to use the price and profit mechanism to meet the energy challenge is disturbing. Moreover, any policy designed substantially to hold down the rate of economic growth will have a serious adverse impact on capital formation and thus be self-fulfilling. It is also vital to encourage the necessary investment in plant and equipment if technological advancement is to continue on a significant scale here and elsewhere. This factor is particularly important in a period during which energy costs have escalated sharply.

The concern of the stagnationists about the lack of availability of new investment opportunities was proved to be completely wrong during the post-World War II years. Total nonresidential fixed investment had declined from $37.0 billion [in 1972 dollars] in 1929 to $20.7 billion in 1939. In the following decades there was an explosive growth in the opportunities for such investments which rose to $127.1 billion in 1977 as shown in Table 1.3. However, this total was still slightly below the peak reached in 1973.

The pessimists could be equally wrong today. It should be noted that an enormous increase in the volume of savings is projected. The concern is not that there will be no increase in savings but that it will not be large enough to finance past rates of economic growth. The shortfall in these estimates is about 15%. A small increase in the savings rate or a small decrease in investment requirements would eliminate the gap. Considering the global nature of the estimates, there is no assurance that there will be a shortfall, nor that if it takes place it will hold down growth rates below the levels that we would otherwise achieve.

The slowdown in population growth and the probable lower rate of increase in productivity suggest that annual rates of economic growth will be lower in the balance of this century than in the past. Such a development would affect both investments and savings. They can be kept in proper balance by market-determined interest rates[50] and tax policies designed to provide adequate incentives to invest and to save.

Growth of Service Industries

Service industries have been increasing sharply in relative importance in terms of employment but only modestly in terms of real gross domestic product as Dr. Fuchs explains in Chapter 6. According to the U.S. Department of Labor, Bureau of Labor Statistics[51], the proportion of nonagricultural employment in the service sector rose from 56.7 percent in 1945 to 70.6 percent in 1976.[52] Table 1.4 compares the percentage for selected years from 1929-76. Because of the lower productivity in many service sectors, this trend is viewed by some observers as a factor holding down future rates of economic growth.

Within the service area, the percentages employed in miscellaneous services and government have increased significantly over the years while the relative proportions in transportation and public utilities have declined.[53]

There is still no indication that the rise in relative employment accounted for by services and government has come to an end. As Victor Fuchs notes, the past increase in government employment has reflected the large growth in areas such as health and education "in which government traditionally has played a role" rather than the muliplication and expansion of government "in accordance with Parkinson's Law." The development of public service jobs to provide earnings for some of the unemployed may expand the relative role of government in the years ahead. Although education probably will decrease in relative importance, medical and legal services continue to increase.

From 1948 to 1973 real product per person engaged in production (so-called labor productivity) rose by 2.9 percent a year for the private domestic business sector. However, for trade the increase was 2.3 percent and for business, domestic, personal, and commercial services only 1.0 percent, while finance and insurance declined by 0.6 percent. On the other hand, the increase for public utilities was 5.0 percent, for communications 5.2 percent, railroads 4.6 percent, nonrail transport 2.9 percent, and real estate 3.0 percent.[54]

Only scattered data are available for productivity in government. One study reported that output per man-hour in the federal government rose by slightly less than 2 percent a year from fiscal 1967 to 1971.[55] It has been pointed out that the increase in total productivity in government enterprises reflected in part the fact that "the low pro-

Table 1.4 Percent of Total Employment Accounted For By Service Industries, Selected Years, 1929-76

	Transportation and Public Utilities	Wholesale and Retail Trade	Finance Insurance & Real Estate	Services	Government	Total
			(Percent of Total Employment)			
1929	12.5	19.5	4.8	11.0	9.8	57.6
1939	9.6	21.0	4.8	11.5	13.0	59.9
1945	9.7	18.1	3.7	10.5	14.7	56.7
1955	8.2	20.8	4.6	12.4	13.6	59.6
1965	6.6	20.9	5.0	14.9	16.6	64.0
1975	5.8	22.1	5.5	18.2	19.1	70.7
1976	5.7	22.3	5.4	18.4	18.8	70.6

SOURCE: U.S. Department of Labor, Bureau of Labor Statistics, *Employment and Earnings*, July 1977, p. 69.

ductivity post office declined in importance while other federal, state, and local enterprises grew."[56]

Transportation, public utilities, and communications have been areas with above-average rates of increase in productivity, due largely to the large-scale application of capital. However, this pattern may be modified in the years ahead. Slower gains in technology and smaller increases in volume could result in a more modest rate of increase in productivity for electric power and gas.

Thus, the rate of increase in productivity in various service areas may be adversely affected by developments already underway. It is unlikely that productivity in service industries will accelerate or even keep pace with the overall advance for the private domestic business economy.

With services accounting for an increasing share of national output such a development would act to slow down somewhat the overall increases in real gross national product. Victor Fuchs projects a growth rate for total output only 0.3 percentage points lower in the 1976-90 period than in the past fifteen years. He concludes in Chapter 6 that "Although output growth will slow, there is no basis for assuming a 'stagnant' economy."

ECONOMIC GROWTH: A MAJOR GOAL

Economic growth must remain a major goal of public policy. Total population will continue to increase despite a slower *rate* of growth. Economic growth is necessary to provide the jobs required by our expanding labor force and to meet the rising expectations of minority groups. In the absence of economic growth, we would experience a steadily increasing and intolerable volume of unemployment. To the extent productivity continued to increase—as it probably would—it would take fewer workers to produce the unchanging volume of output with a further aggravation of the unemployment problem.

With zero economic growth, the ability to improve the economic position of the underprivileged and minority groups would be severely inhibited. Progress is made most easily in achieving this goal when the size of the pie is increased. Under conditions of zero economic growth, there would be increasingly severe social tensions as efforts were made to redistribute the existing pie and to bring disadvantaged groups into fuller equality in the economy. It is ironic that the advocates of zero economic growth present their clarion call at a time when we are setting up a series of very costly priorities. There is the need to replenish the nation's housing stock, to improve the lot of low income groups, to improve mass transportation, to clean up the environment, et cetera.

A stagnating economy, which experiences a continuing increase in the size of its population, must, as a matter of simple arithmetic, inevitably undergo a decline in the average level of living. Against a background of rising expectations, such a development would create enormous social pressures. But the options also would be severely limited because they would require a major redistribution of income. As past experience has shown, government has the greatest flexibility in its programs, when it can finance its actions by using part of an expanding national product.

A no-growth economy also would curtail our ability to reduce pollution. Active pollution abatement necessitates a substantial investment of resources. If we wish to make the required investment in pollution control without lowering our current level of consumption, we will have to pursue a growth policy that expands our production possibilities sufficiently to maintain current levels of living as well as to invest in pollution abatement equipment. At the same time, we must recognize that diversion of investment for this purpose will act to hold down the overall rate of economic growth.

A word of caution is in order. The goal should not be a frenetic pace of economic growth without regard to economic consequences. This was the problem in earlier days in our economy with an accompanying deterioration in the quality of life. We must strike a balance between the needs for current consumption and saving and investment to develop future higher levels of consumption. It should be clear that the growth rates must be at sustainable levels and not fired up to excessively high rates by stimulants, which at best can have only a short-term leavening effect, followed by a longer-term destabilizing effect as the stimulant wears off.

The best way to accomplish this goal is not through a government-directed economy but rather to create an economic environment in which private decisions to save and to invest are encouraged. Such an economic environment requires less interference with the operation of the price system. The variety of price controls imposed over oil and natural gas to meet the energy crisis provides an outstanding illustration of the wrong approach. Moreover, action must be taken to reduce or to rationalize the regulatory activities and paper work which are adding such a large cost to business and diverting resources which could be devoted to achieving economic growth.

Encouragement of private initiatives should be the goal of public policy. And if the result is large profits, so be it. If some resources become relatively scarce they will command a premium in the market place in the form of higher prices. This will discourage high utilization rates as well as encourage further production, substitution of other resources, and emphasis on research. Economic incentives induce people to make better use of resources as they become increasingly scarce. Profits play a crucial role in that they usually induce the additional expansion required to bring forth increased supplies. This availability acts to hold down prices and to dampen down future profit rates. An outstanding illustration of this development is found in the large scale entry by many big companies into the chemical industry during the 1950s and 1960s with the resulting decline in profit rates in the late 1960s.[57]

The international consequences of a no-growth economy in the United States also are of vital importance. We are a major purchaser of goods throughout the world. A stagnant market in the U.S. would abort growth possibilities for many developing countries and would have a severe impact on the economies of other industrial countries. The growing unemployment here would aggravate the problem as political pressures mounted to restrict imports in order to provide jobs for our own unemployed. Despite the mountain of affirmative evidence, we have not developed the economic sophistication to understand the full benefits derived from international specialization of production and trade. The unemployed workers and union leaders couldn't care less.

The international political consequences which would develop if the Communist countries continued to expand while we and our allies are stagnating also should not be underestimated. Some European countries would fall like ripe plums into the Communist camp. At the same time our own world position would be undermined.

The combination of the factors discussed above far outweighs the case of those who argue that environmental consideration call for a no-growth policy. Our national policy should be to encourage economic growth and to meet environmental problems by imposing penalties upon polluters. We can have both a cleaner environment and the benefits that flow from economic growth.

NOTES

1. Alvin Hansen, *Fiscal Policy and Business Cycles* (New York: Norton, 1941), p.353.

2. For an attempt to measure economic welfare, see William Nordhaus and James Tobin, *Economic Growth* (New York: National Bureau of Economic Research, 1972).

3. Hansen, *Fiscal Policy and Business Cycles,* pp.42-43.

4. Asher Achinstein, *Introduction to Business Cycles* (New York: Crowell, 1950), p.384.

5. "Economic Progress and Declining Economic Growth" in American Economic Association's, *Readings in Business Cycle Theory* (Philadelphia, Pa.: Blakiston Co., 1944), p.377.

6. James A. Estey, *Business Cycles,* Second Edition (New york: Prentice-Hall, 1950), p.136-37.

7 Hansen, Fiscal Policy and Business Cycles, p.45.

8. U.S. Commissioner of Labor, *First Annual Report* (Washington, D.C., March 1886), pp.242-43.

9. Harold Vatter, *The U.S. Economy in the 1950's* (New York: Norton, 1963), p.8.

10. U.S. Department of Commerce, Bureau of the Census, *Historical Statistics of the United States, Colonial Times to 1970,* Part 1 (Washington, D.C., 1975), p.49, and *Statistical Abstract of the United States: 1976* (Washington, D.C., 1976), p.51.

11. *The Wall Street Journal,* 29 July 1977, pp.1, 20.

12. U.S. Department of Commerce, Bureau of the Census, *Statistical Abstract of the United States: 1966* (Washington, D.C., 1966), p.63.

13. "America in the Sixties," *Fortune* (New York: Harper and Row, 1960), p.4.

14. An indication of the growth of research and development is found in the increased number of scientists and engineers in American industry—from 557,000 in 1950 to 1,595,000 in 1970.

15. *Statistical Abstract of the United States: 1976,* p.568.

16. George L. Bach, *Economics,* Ninth Edition (Englewood Cliffs, N.J.: Prentice-Hall, 1977), p.304.

17. The U.S. Bureau of the Census has concluded that "the population of the United States will continue to grow throughout the remainder of the twentieth century at rates which could fall below the current low rate and which are unlikely to reach the relatively high rate of the 1950s." See U.S. Department of Commerce *Current Population Reports*, Series P-25, no. 601, "Projections of the Population of the United States: 1975 to 2050" (Washington, D.C.: Bureau of the Census, October 1975), p.2.

18. U.S. Department of Commerce, Series II estimates *Current Population Reports*, Series P-25, no. 704, "Projections of the Population of the United States: 1977 to 2050" (Washington, D.C.: Bureau of the Census, July 1977), pp.4, 14.

19. Howard N. Fullerton, Jr. and Paul O. Flaim, "New Labor Force Projections to 1990," *Special Labor Force Report 197* (Washington, D.C.: U.S. Bureau of Labor Statistics, 1977), p.3.

20. *Economic Report of the President* (Washington, D.C.: Council of Economic Advisers, January 1977), pp.86-87.

21. *The Wall Street Journal*, 26 September 1977, p.2. Several corporations had announced earlier increases in retirement ages: Westinghouse Electric Co. in June 1977 *(New York Times,* 30 June 1977) and Connecticut General Insurance Corp. in August 1977 *(New York Times,* 1 August 1977).

22. *Business Week,* 20 December 1976.

23. *New York Times,* 9 August 1977.

24. *Key Elements of a National Energy Strategy* (New York: Committee for Economic Development, June 1977), p.8.

25. Edward J. Mitchell, *U.S. Energy Policy: A Primer* (Washington: American Enterprise Institute, June 1974), p.5.

26. For a review of developments in solar energy, see *Solar Energy, Progress and Promise* (Washington, D.C.: Council on Environmental Quality, April 1978).There are substantial geothermal deposits that are below the Rocky Mountain states. Efforts by oil and power companies to use this form of power are in motion. *(New York Times,* 4 January 1978).

27. It has been reported that Rockwell International "estimates that it will burn 1,000 tons of trash a year and that this will produce as much heat as 15 million cubic feet of natural gas and as much cooling capacity as one million kilowatt hours of electricity. In fiscal 1978, the pollution-free trash burner will save Rockwell $102,800 on electricity, $42,700 on natural gas and $14,560 in trash-hauling fees." *The Wall Street Journal,* 22 September 1977, p.1.

28. *Federal Energy Administration Regulation, Report of The Presidential Task Force,* ed.

Paul W. MacAvoy (Washington, D.C.: American Enterprise Institute for Public Policy Research, 1977), Preface.

29. When U.S. Steel agreed to spend over $150 million on water pollution control equipment at its Gary, Indiana, steel plant, Edward L. Smith, a company vice-president, noted that " . . . the more we put in environmental pollution equipment, the less we have to spend on modernization." *Wall Street Journal*, 11 August 1977.

30. Frank W. Segel and Betsy C. Dunlap, "Capital Expenditures by Business for Pollution Abatement, 1976 and Planned 1977," *Survey of Current Business*, June 1977, p.13.

31. Edward F. Denison, "Effects of Selected Changes in the International and Human Environment Upon Output Per Unit of Input," *Survey of Current Business*, January 1978, p.41.

32. "Ecology's Missing Price Tag," *Wall Street Journal*, 10 August 1976.

33. Harold J. Barnett, "Natural Environment and Growth," in Joint Economic Committee, U.S. Congress, *U.S. Economic Growth from 1976 to 1986: Prospects, Problems, and Patterns*, vol. 10, *The Quality of Economic Growth* (Washington, D.C., 1977), p.1. A Bureau of Labor Statistics projection of productivity trends to 1985 reached a similar conclusion. Ronald E. Kutscher, Jerome A. Mark, and John R. Norsworthy, "The Productivity Slowdown and The Outlook to 1985," *Monthly Labor Review*, May 1977, p.7.

34. Jules Backman, "Economic Growth, Standards of Living, and Quality of Life," in *Tomorrow's American*, ed. Samuel Sandmel (New York: Oxford University Press, 1977), Chapter 4.

35. Lester C. Thurow, "The Implications of Zero Economic Growth," *Challenge*, March-April 1977, p.43.

36. In 1967, total per capita consumption of beer was only 5 percent higher than in 1950. However, the number of bottles per gallon had increased by 408 percent because of the shift to throw-away bottles. Barry Commoner, "Energy, Environment and Economics," in *Energy: The Policy Issues*, ed. Gary D. Eppen (Chicago: The University of Chicago Press, 1975), p.29.

37. This problem first emerged into public focus with the publication of the Paley Report, named for its chairman, in 1952. The President's Materials Policy Commission reported that the pattern of rising demand and shrinking resources gave cause for concern about the adequacy of material resources. However, no action was taken on the recommendations of this study group. *Resources for Freedom* (Washington, D.C.: President's Materials Policy Commission, 1952).

38. *Survey of Current Business,* December 1973, p.1. See also *Economic Report of the President* (Washington, D.C.: Council of Economic Advisers, February 1974), p.63, and "Managing in a Shortage Economy," *Business Week,* 10 November 1973, pp.150-54.

39. Donella H. Meadows, Dennis L. Meadows, Jørgen Randers, and William W. Behrens III, *The Limits to Growth* (New York: Universe Books, 1972), p.126.

40. See, for example, Bach, *Economics,* pp.612-14.

41. *Time,* April 26, 1976, p.56.

42. Solomon Fabricant, "The Growth of the American Economy, 1776-2001," in *Business and the American Economy, 1776-2001,* ed. Jules Backman (New York: New York University Press), 1976, p.50.

43. It has been estimated that $3 trillion of oil, natural gas, and mineral resources, including manganese, nickel, copper, cobalt, and uranium, can be recovered from the oceans. *World Mineral Supplies* (New York: Editoral Research Reports, 28 May 1976), p.400. See also U.S. Senate Committee on Interior and Insular Affairs, Subcommittee on Minerals, Materials and Fuels, *Mineral Resources of the Deep Seabed* (Washington, D.C., 1973).

44. Nathan Rosenberg, "Thinking About Technology Policy For The Coming Decade," in *U.S. Economic Growth from 1976 to 1986: Prospects, Problems, and Patterns,* vol. 9 (Washington, D.C.: Joint Economic Committee, U.S. Congress, 1977), pp.1-32.

45. *Minerals Yearbook 1974* (Washington, D.C.: U.S. Department of the Interior, 1976), pp.664-65.

46. National Academy of Sciences, *Mineral Resources and the Environment* (Washington, D.C.: National Academy of Sciences Printing Office, 1975), p.1.

47. *The Capital Needs and Savings Potential of the U.S. Economy: Projections Through 1985* (New York: New York Stock Exchange, September 1974), p.11.

48. *Economic Report of the President* (Washington, D.C.: Council of Economic Advisers, January 1976), p.46.

49. Barry Bosworth, James S. Duesenberry, and Andrew S. Carron, *Capital Needs in the Seventies* (Washington, D.C.: Brookings Institution, 1975). Professor George A. Doyle has raised some questions about the Brookings study, particularly the assumption that we will have a "full employment surplus" in the federal budget. See *Foundations For A National Policy To Preserve Enterprise In The 1980's* (Washington, D.C.: Subcommittee on Economic Growth and Stabilization of the Joint Economic Committee, U.S. Congress, 1977), pp.12-13.

50. Martin S. Feldstein, "National Saving in the United States," in *Capital For Produc-*

tivity and Jobs, ed. Eli Shapiro and William L. White (Englewood Cliffs, N.J.: Prentice-Hall, 1976), pp.146-47.

51. U.S. Department of Labor, Bureau of Labor Statistics, *Employment and Earnings,* July 1977, p.69.

52. Edward F. Denison has estimated that the service sector increased in relative importance from 49.8 percent in 1929 to 53.6 percent in 1948 and 63.8 percent in 1969. He used a different definition for persons engaged in production, namely, "the sum of the numbers of full-time equivalent employees and active proprietors of unincorporated businesses." Edward F. Denison, "The Shift to Services and the Rate of Productivity Change," *Survey of Current Business,* October 1973, pp.20, 21. Victor Fuchs reported an increase from 46.0 percent in 1948 to 60.7 percent in 1976. See Chapter 6, Table 6.1.

53. Includes educational, medical, legal, laundries, hotels, motion pictures, advertising, nonprofit research, building services, engineering, and architectural.

54. John W. Kendrick, *Morgan Guaranty Survey,* May 1976, and *Postwar Productivity Trends in the United States* (New York: National Bureau of Economic Research, 1973).

55. *Measuring and Enhancing Productivity in the Federal Government, Summary Report* (Washington: Joint Federal Productivity Project, 1973).

56. Kutscher, Mark and Norsworthy, "Productivity Slowdown," p.5.

57. See Jules Backman, *The Economics of the Chemical Industry* (Washington, D.C.: Manufacturing Chemists Association, 1970), pp.67-75.

TWO

Economic Growth or Stagnation:

The Role of Technology

Edwin Mansfield
Professor of Economics
University of Pennsylvania

INTRODUCTION

In recent years, there has been a growing uneasiness among some economists concerning our nation's future rate of economic growth, here defined as the rate of growth of output per capita. This uneasiness manifested itself recently at the Fifth World Congress of the International Economic Association (1977), which was dedicated entirely to the topic of economic growth. Moses Abramowitz, the Congress's first principal speaker, concluded that "the importance of the essentially transitory influences in postwar development and the fact that these have now weakened and, in some cases, disappeared make the prospects for an early renewal of the postwar growth drive uncertain and dubious."[1]

In this chapter, the role of technology in determining our future rate of economic growth is discussed. Since this is a very broad topic and space is limited, I shall have to be both selective and brief. First, I shall outline a summary of what is known about the contribution of technology to economic growth. Then I shall describe three recent developments that have aroused public concern: the slackening of U.S. productivity growth, the reduced share of our gross national product going for research and development, and the apparent narrowing of the U.S. technological lead over other countries. Next, I'll take up the question of whether or not the United States may be underinvesting in civilian technology, and discuss the relevant policy alternatives. Finally, turning to the future, some comments are offered regarding the current state of technological forecasting techniques, as well as concerning some warnings about the rate of technological advance and productivity increase in the United States.

THE ROLE OF TECHNOLOGICAL CHANGE IN ECONOMIC GROWTH

Technological change consists of advances in knowledge concerning the industrial and agricultural arts. Such advances result in new and improved processes and products, as well as new techniques of organization and management. The fact that technological change plays an important role in permitting and stimulating economic growth seems self-evident. But when one wants to go beyond such bland generalizations to a quantitative summary of the contribution of technological change to the rate of economic growth, a number of basic difficulties are encountered. For one thing, it is hard to separate the effects on economic growth of technological change from those of investment in physical capital, since, to be used, new technology frequently must be embodied in physical capital—new machines and plant. For example, a numerically controlled machine tool (or control mechanism) must be built to take full advantage of some advances in the technology related to machine tools. Nor can the effects of technological change easily be separated from those of education, since the social returns from increased education are enhanced by technological change, and the rate of technological change is influenced by the extent and nature of our society's investment in education.

Despite these and other problems, economists have tried to obtain quantitative measures of the importance of technological change in American economic growth. In a seminal article published in 1957, Robert Solow attempted to estimate the rate of technological change in the nonfarm U.S. economy during 1909 to 1949.[2] His findings indicated that, for the period as a whole, the average rate of technological change was about 1.5 percent per year. Based on these findings he concluded that about 90 percent of the increase in output per capita during that period was attributable to technological change, whereas only a minor percentage of the increase was due to increases in the amount of capital employed per worker.

Solow's measure of the effects of technological change also included the effects of whatever inputs were excluded, such as increases in education or improved health and nutrition of workers, as well as economies of scale, improved allocation of resources, and changes in product mix. To obtain a purer measure, Edward Denison[3] attempted to include many factors—for example, changes in labor quality associated with increases in schooling—that had been omitted, largely or completely, by Solow and others, such as Abramowitz and Solomon Fabricant.[4] Since it was relatively comprehensive, Denison's study resulted in a lower residual increase in output unexplained by the inputs he included than did Solow. Specifically, Denison concluded that the *advance of knowledge*—his term for the residual—was responsible for about 40 percent of the total increase in national income per person employed during 1929-57 in the United States.

Besides trying to estimate the contribution of technological change to the growth rate of the entire economy, economists have also investigated the effects on the rates of productivity increase of individual firms or industries of the amounts spent on research and development (R & D). The results provide reasonably persuasive evidence that R & D has had a significant effect on the rate of productivity increase in the industries and over the time periods that have been studied. Minasian[5] and I[6] found that, in chemicals and petroleum, a firm's rate of productivity increase was directly related to its expenditures on R & D. In agriculture, Griliches found that, holding other inputs constant, output was related in a statistically significant way to the amount spent on research and extension. More recently, Griliches, Nadiri and Bitros, as well as Terleckyj have provided much additional evidence on this score.[7]

In addition to these statistical studies, many valuable case studies have been carried out to shed light on the ways in which new technology has affected various aspects and sectors of our economy. For example, studies have been made of the economic effects of petroleum cracking innovations and of electronics innovations, among others.[8]

These studies show the major role played by new technologies in determining the size, viability, and profitability of particular industries and firms, as well as their competitiveness in international trade.

Of course, all of these studies—both those at the national level and those at the industry and firm level, and both those relying on econometric techniques and those that are essentially case studies— have an impressive number and variety of limitations. (Since I have commented elsewhere at length on these limitations, I shall not do so here.[9]) Nonetheless, it seems to me that they demonstrate beyond any reasonable doubt that technological change is one of the principal factors, perhaps the most important factor, determining the rate of economic growth in the aggregate economy as well as the rate of productivity increase in individual firms and industries.

THE SLACKENING OF U.S. PRODUCTIVITY GROWTH

There has been considerable concern among policymakers (both in the public and private sectors) concerning the reduction in recent years of the rate of productivity growth in the United States. One important productivity measure is output per man-hour. According to the Bureau of Labor Statistics, output per man-hour (in the private sector) grew at an average annual rate of 3.2 percent from 1947 to 1966, but at an average annual rate of 1.6 percent from 1967 to 1976.[10] In part, the slower rate of increase of labor productivity in the later period was due to the fact that this period contained two recessions; thus, the slower rate of productivity increase was in part a cyclical phenomenon. But this is only part of the story.

Another important measure of productivity is total factor productivity, defined as real output per unit of total factor input. Since both labor and nonhuman factor inputs are unadjusted for quality changes, the rate of increase of total factor productivity reflects changes in the average quality of resource inputs, as well as changes in technology, changes in efficiency, and other factors discussed below. Table 2.1 shows that the average annual rate of increase of total factor productivity fell after 1966. Whereas total factor productivity increased by 2.5 percent per year between 1948 and 1966, it increased by 1.1 percent per year between 1966 and 1969, and by 2.1 percent per year between

Table 2.1 Productivity Changes in the U.S. Private Domestic Economy, 1948-73

	1948-66	1948-53	1953-57	1957-60	1960-66	1966-69	1969-73[a]
				(average annual percentage rate of change)			
Total factor productivity (private domestic economy)	2.5	2.7	1.9	2.2	2.8	1.1	2.1
Output per man-hour							
Agriculture	5.6	6.4	4.1	5.9	5.8	6.7	5.3
Mining	4.6	5.2	3.3	4.7	3.7	1.8	0.2
Contract construction	2.0	4.4	3.2	1.5	-0.5	-0	-0.5
Manufacturing	2.9	3.7	2.2	2.2	3.6	2.7	4.5
Transportation	3.7	2.2	3.1	3.0	4.8	2.2	4.5
Communication	5.5	5.4	3.6	7.6	5.7	4.6	4.1
Electric and gas utilities	6.1	7.6	6.3	5.4	5.1	4.4	1.0
Trade	2.9	2.5	2.7	1.9	3.9	2.1	2.3
Finance	2.1	1.5	2.7	1.5	2.6	-0.4	0.2
Services	1.2	0.5	1.2	1.1	1.7	0.4	1.0

SOURCE: John Kendrick, "Productivity Trends and Prospects," in *U.S. Economic Growth from 1976 to 1986* (Washington, D.C.: Joint Economic Committee of Congress, 1 October 1976), vol. 1, p. 19.
[a]preliminary.

1969 and 1973. Table 2.1 also shows that output per man-hour increased at a slower rate during 1966-73 than during 1948-66 in most sectors of the economy, as well as in the economy as a whole.[11]

According to the Bureau of Labor Statistics, two of the major factors responsible for this slowdown were the end of the shift of labor from farm to nonfarm employment and the increase in the proportion of youths and women in the labor force. Because productivity was generally higher in nonfarm than farm employment, the movement of workers off the farms tended for many years to raise productivity. As this movement has abated, productivity might have been expected to increase more slowly. According to the Bureau, this factor alone may have been responsible for 0.3-0.4 percentage points of the difference between the average annual rate of productivity increase in 1947-66 and that in 1966-73. Output per man-hour tends to be relatively low among new entrants into the labor force and among women. During the late 1960s, new entrants and women increased as a percentage of the labor force. According to the Bureau, this change in labor force composition may have been responsible for 0.2-0.3 percentage points of the difference between the average annual rate of productivity increase in 1947-66 and that in 1966-73.[12] Both Denison and George Perry, in their analyses of the causes of the slowdown, agree that this factor was very important.[13]

Another factor that has been cited in this regard is a change in the capital-labor ratio. According to Christensen, Cummings, and Jorgensen, there was a decrease in the rate of growth of the capital-labor ratio during the 1960s.[14] Still another reason given for the productivity slowdown is the shift of national output toward services and away from goods. According to William Nordhaus, this shift in the composition of national output is responsible for much of the slowdown.[15] However, Michael Grossman and Victor Fuchs, and the Bureau of Labor Statistics, among others, are skeptical of this proposition.[16]

Still others like John Kendrick have attributed some of the slowdown in productivity increase to the reduction in the rate of increase of intangible capital due to the decrease in the percentage of gross national product devoted to R & D during the late 1960s and early 1970s.[17] In the following section, we shall look in some detail at the level of R & D expenditures in the U.S. in recent years. At this point, it is sufficient to say that in the U.S., R & D expenditures decreased, as a percentage of gross national product, from 2.99 percent in 1964 to 2.25 percent in 1976. To my knowledge, no study has been carried out to determine how much of the slowdown in productivity growth could be due to this factor. In part, the lack of such studies is undoubtedly attributable to the great theoretical and empirical problems they would present.

REDUCED SHARE OF GNP ALLOCATED FOR RESEARCH AND DEVELOPMENT

The National Science Foundation (N.S.F.) publishes detailed data concerning the size and characteristics of our nation's expenditures on R & D. Table 2.2 shows the changes during 1960-74 in the amount spent (in current and constant dollars) on R & D, as well as the changes in the percent of GNP devoted to research and development. The constant dollar figures are very crude, since they are based on the use of the GNP deflator. Unfortunately, the problems in constructing a price index for R & D appear so formidable that N.S.F. has been forced to adopt this procedure. Conclusions indicated by Table 2.2 follow.

First, the percentage of gross national product devoted to R & D fell from 2.99 percent in 1964 to 2.29 percent in 1974. This decline occurred almost continuously from 1964 to 1974, each year showing a somewhat lower percentage than the previous year. Moreover, more recent data indicate that this percentage was slightly lower in 1976 than in 1974.

Second, Table 2.2 indicates that, when inflation is taken into account, our nation's expenditures on R & D have remained essentially constant from 1966 to 1974. Moreover, according to more recent figures, it appears that real R & D expenditures in 1976 were no higher than in 1966. As noted earlier, constant dollar figures should be viewed with caution, since the deflator that is used is extremely crude. Nonetheless, it seems to be generally accepted that these figures are in the right ball park, in the sense that no appreciable increase in real R & D expenditures took place during this period.

Third, the constancy of real R & D expenditures during 1966-74

Table 2.2 Expenditures on Research and Development, United States, 1960-74

Year	R & D expenditures as a percent of Gross National Product	R & D expenditures (billions of dollars)[b]		R & D expenditures (billions of 1967 dollars)			
		Current dollars	1967 dollars	Federal government	Industry	Colleges, universities	Other nonprofit institutions
1960	2.70	13.6	15.4	10.0	5.1	0.2	0.2
1961	2.75	14.3	16.1	10.4	5.3	0.2	0.2
1962	2.75	15.4	17.1	11.0	5.7	0.2	0.2
1963	2.90	17.1	18.8	12.3	6.0	0.2	0.2
1964	2.99	18.9	20.4	13.6	6.4	0.3	0.2
1965	2.93	20.1	21.3	13.8	6.9	0.3	0.3
1966	2.92	21.9	22.6	14.4	7.6	0.3	0.3
1967	2.92	23.2	23.2	14.4	8.1	0.3	0.3
1968	2.86	24.7	23.7	14.4	8.6	0.4	0.3
1969	2.76	25.7	23.6	13.7	9.2	0.4	0.3
1970	2.66	26.0	22.6	12.8	9.1	0.4	0.3
1971	2.53	26.7	22.2	12.5	9.0	0.4	0.3
1972	2.45	28.4	22.9	12.8	9.3	0.5	0.4
1973	2.35	30.4	23.2	12.6	9.8	0.5	0.4
1974[a]	2.29	32.0	22.1	11.7	9.6	0.5	0.3

SOURCE: *Science Indicators, 1974* (Washington, D.C.: National Science Foundation, 1975).
[a]Preliminary.
[b]Differences may exist in total due to rounding.

conceals two quite different trends: whereas federally financed R & D was declining from $14.4 billion in 1966 to $11.7 billion in 1974, the industry-financed total was increasing from $7.6 billion in 1966 to $9.6 billion in 1974. In large part, the reduction in federally financed R & D was due to the winding down of the space program and the reduction (in constant dollars) of defense R & D expenditures. Although defense and space R & D have some "spillover" effect on civilian technology, such declines would be expected to have less effect on the rate of economic growth than if commensurate declines were to occur in privately financed R & D.[18]

Fourth, Table 2.2 indicates that, while industry-financed R & D expenditures (in constant dollars) increased during 1966-74, the rate of increase was less than during 1960-66. Indeed, between 1969 and 1972, they did not increase at all. One possible reason for the slower rate of increase of industrial R & D expenditures (in real terms) during the late 1960s and early 1970s was that the profitability of such expenditures may have tended to stabilize, or even to fall off, during this period. For one of the nation's largest firms, we found in a recent study that the private rate of return from its investment in new technology tended to be lower during the late 1960s and early 1970s than during the early 1960s.[19] This seems to be the only direct evidence on this score.

Some observers and policymakers view the developments shown in Table 2.2 with alarm. For example, in its draft study on U.S. technology policy, the Office of the Assistant Secretary of Commerce for Science and Technology cites these developments in connection with its stated concern that there may be an underinvestment in R & D in the United States.[20] Of course, these figures by themselves cannot prove or disprove that such an underinvestment exists. As we shall see in a subsequent section, data of quite a different sort are needed to deal adequately with this question.

NARROWING OF THE U.S. TECHNOLOGICAL LEAD

Still another development in this area that has been the object of considerable concern in both the private and public sectors is the apparent reduction of the U.S. technological lead over other countries.

The available evidence, which is fragmentary at best, suggests that, for a long time, U.S. technology has tended to lead that of other industrialized countries. For example, scattered impressionistic evidence prior to 1850 indicates such a technology gap existed in many fields. And after 1850, the available quantitative evidence suggests that total factor productivity was higher in the United States than in Europe, that the United States had a strong export position in technically progressive industries, and that Europeans tended to imitate American techniques. The existence of such a gap in the nineteenth century would not be surprising, since this was a heyday of American invention. Of course, the United States did not lead in all fields, but it appears that we held a technological lead in many important areas of manufacturing.[21]

In the 1960s, Europeans expressed their uneasiness and worry over the technology gap. They claimed that superior know-how stemming from scientific and technical achievements in the United States had permitted American companies to obtain large shares of European markets in fields like aircraft, space equipment, computers, and other electronic products. In 1966, Italy's Foreign Minister Amintore Fanfani went so far as to call for a "technological Marshall Plan" to speed the flow of American technology across the Atlantic. In response to such concern, the Organization for Economic Cooperation and Development (OECD) made a major study of the nature of the technology gap. It concluded that a large gap existed in computers and some electronic components, but that no general or fundamental gap existed in pharmaceuticals, bulk plastics, iron and steel, machine tools (other than numerically controlled machine tools), nonferrous metals (other than tantalum and titanium), and scientific instruments (other than electronic test and measuring instruments). The OECD studies suggested that the American technological lead was largest in the relatively research-intensive sectors of the economy.[22]

During the 1970s, observers in the United States have expressed increasing concern that this technological lead is being reduced. For example, the 1975 annual report of the National Science Board contains a study suggesting that the percentage of major innovations originating in the United States fell substantially from 1953 to 1967 and has remained relatively stable since 1968 as shown in Table 2.3. Needless to say, there is a host of conceptual and statistical difficulties with

Table 2.3   Major Technological Innovations, by Selected Countries, 1953-73

Period	United States	United Kingdom	West Germany	Japan	France	Total[a]
			(percentage of total)			
1953-55	75	14	6	0	5	100
1956-58	82	9	5	0	5	100
1959-61	68	21	2	2	7	100
1962-64	66	17	5	12	0	100
1965-67	55	23	12	8	3	100
1968-70	57	19	8	13	4	100
1971-73	58	16	9	10	8	100

SOURCE: *Science Indicators, 1974* (Washington, D.C.: National Science Foundation, 1975), p. 165.
[a]Individual figures may not sum to 100 because of rounding.

measures of this sort, as the National Science Board recognizes. And to some extent, a diminution in our technological lead would have been expected as countries like Japan and West Germany got back on their feet after the war. Nonetheless, to the extent that these indicators are valid and their past trends continue, they may portend problems in international markets for some industries that have contributed significantly to our trade balance.[23]

Concern is also being expressed in many quarters regarding the slow rate of productivity growth in the United States relative to other major countries. As shown in Table 2.4, the percentage gain in output per man-hour during 1960-74 was smaller in the United States than in France, West Germany, Japan, or the United Kingdom. Indeed, the Japanese percentage productivity gain was over four times that of the United States during this period. If comparisons are made of rates of increase of total factor productivity rather than of output per man-hour, the results are the same. Christensen, Cummings, and Jorgensen found that, during 1960-73, the rate of increase of total factor productivity was lower in the U.S. than in any other country included in their analysis (Canada, France, West Germany, Italy, Japan, Korea, Netherlands, United Kingdom).[24] Of course, it must be recognized in any comparisons of this sort that other countries' productivity *levels* tend to be lower than that in the United States. But rightly or wrong-

Table 2.4   Output per Man-hour in Manufacturing Industries, Selected Countries, 1960-74

Year	United States	Japan	France (1960 = 100)	West Germany	United Kingdom
1960	100.0	100.0	100.0	100.0	100.0
1961	102.5	113.1	104.7	105.4	100.8
1962	108.3	118.1	109.5	112.2	103.3
1963	112.7	127.6	116.0	118.1	108.9
1964	118.0	144.6	121.8	127.3	116.8
1965	122.7	150.7	128.8	136.1	120.3
1966	124.3	165.9	137.8	141.6	124.6
1967	124.2	190.5	145.6	150.6	130.2
1968	130.2	214.5	162.2	162.0	138.9
1969	133.3	247.6	168.0	171.4	140.8
1970	134.0	279.0	176.4	175.8	142.1
1971	143.1	289.0	185.6	184.2	148.7
1972	151.2	312.2	198.1	195.9	154.8
1973	159.4	368.8	209.6	209.9	165.6
1974[a]	160.5	380.8	221.1	215.1	165.8

SOURCE: P. Capdevielle and A. Neef, "Productivity and Unit Labor Costs in the United States and Abroad," *Monthly Labor Review* (July 1975).
[a]Preliminary.

ly, comparisons of this sort have led to concern over our nation's technological position *vis-à-vis* other countries.

Still another development that has led to such concern is the fact, shown in Table 2.5, that, while R & D expenditures have been decreasing as a percentage of gross national product in the United States, they have been increasing in other countries, such as Japan, West Germany, and the Soviet Union. However, two points should be noted concerning these figures. First, as the National Science Foundation points out, the data for the Soviet Union are not comparable with those for the United States, and may be overestimated relative to the U.S.[25] Second, although the percent of GNP devoted to R & D has increased in these other countries relative to that in the United States, the U.S. percentage is still higher than in most other countries. The only country with a considerably higher percentage is the Soviet Union, where the comparability of the figures is dubious.[26]

Table 2.5 R & D Expenditures as a Percent of Gross National Product, Selected Countries, 1961-74

Year	United States	France	West Germany	United Kingdom	Japan	Soviet Union
1961	2.75	1.38	1.08	2.69	n.a.	n.a.
1962	2.75	1.43	1.23	n.a.	n.a.	2.18
1963	2.90	1.53	1.38	n.a.	1.25	2.37
1964	2.99	1.78	1.54	2.62	n.a.	2.42
1965	2.93	1.99	1.70	n.a.	n.a.	2.40
1966	2.92	2.07	1.78	2.79	n.a.	2.42
1967	2.92	2.16	1.94	2.75	1.34	2.55
1968	2.86	2.11	1.93	2.70	n.a.	n.a.
1969	2.76	1.96	1.99	2.73	1.50	2.82
1970	2.66	1.88	2.12	n.a.	n.a.	2.73
1971	2.53	1.87	2.29	n.a.	1.65	2.79
1972	2.45	1.82	2.37	n.a.	1.89	3.04
1973	2.35	1.73	2.36	n.a.	1.92	3.10
1974[a]	2.29	n.a.	2.41	n.a.	n.a.	3.06

SOURCE: *Science Indicators, 1974* (Washington D.C.: National Science Foundation, 1975), p. 154.
[a]Preliminary.

IS THERE AN UNDERINVESTMENT IN INDUSTRIAL INNOVATION IN THE UNITED STATES?

For the past ten or fifteen years, a number of economists in the United States have suspected that we may be underinvesting in civilian technology.[27] On purely theoretical grounds, one cannot prove that such an underinvestment exists. There are several important factors, related to the inappropriability, uncertainty, and indivisibility of R & D, that seem likely to promote an underinvestment in R & D by the private sector. But these factors may be offset, partially or fully, by oligopolistic emphasis on nonprice competition, by existing government programs, or by other factors. Thus, on a priori grounds, it is impossible to say with any reasonable degree of certainty whether there is an underinvestment in various types of civilian technology.[28]

To obtain clues as to whether or not there is such an underinvestment (and if so, where it may be most severe), economists have attempted to estimate the social rate of return from investments in various kinds of new civilian technology. These estimates provide some idea of what society has received from such investments in the past. Of course, there is a host of problems in measuring the social benefits from new technology. Any innovation, particularly a major one, has effects on many firms and industries, and it obviously is hard to evaluate each one and to sum them up properly. Nonetheless, economists have devised techniques that should provide at least rough estimates of the social rate of return from particular innovations, assuming that the innovations are essentially resource-saving in nature.[29]

The earliest studies of this sort were carried out concerning agricultural R & D. Although only a few such studies were made, notably by Griliches, Peterson, and also by Schmitz and Seckler, the results were quite consistent in the sense that they all indicated that the rate of return from agricultural R & D in the United States has tended to be high.[30] Until recently, no such estimates were made for industries other than agriculture. To help fill this gap, my coworkers and I estimated the social rate of return from the investments in seventeen industrial innovations, which occurred in a variety of industries. Most of these innovations were of average or routine importance, not major breakthroughs. The results indicate that the median social rate of return from the investments in these innovations was 56 percent, a very high figure. The median private rate of return was 25 percent (before taxes).[31]

In addition, my colleagues and I obtained data regarding the returns from the innovative activities (from 1960 to 1972) of one of America's largest firms. For each year, this firm has made a careful inventory of the technological innovations arising from its R & D and related activities, and it has made detailed estimates of the effect of each of these innovations on its profit stream. We computed the average private rate of return from this firm's total investment in innovative activities during 1960-72, the result being 19 percent, which is not too different from the median private rate of return given above. Also, we estimated lower bounds for the social rate of return from the firm's investment, and found that they were about double its private rate of return, which also agrees with the results given above.[32]

All of the rates of return cited so far are average rates of return.

That is, they are the average rates of return from all of the amounts spent to obtain the relevant new technology. For many purposes, a more important measure is the marginal rate of return, which is the rate of return from an additional dollar spent. This is the measure that is most relevant in determining whether there is an underinvestment in civilian technology. If the marginal social rate of return from investments in civilian technology is higher than the marginal social rate of return from using the extra resources in other ways, more resources should be devoted to civilian technology. Thus, a very high marginal rate of return from investments in civilian technology is a sign of an underinvestment in civilian R & D.

Based on econometric techniques, a number of studies have estimated the marginal rate of return from various kinds of R & D. My own studies indicated that the marginal rate of return was about 40 percent or more in the petroleum industry and about 30 percent in the chemical industry if technical change was capital embodied (but much less if it was disembodied).[33] Minasian's study indicated about a 50 percent marginal rate of return on investment in R & D in the chemical industry.[34] In agriculture, Griliches found that the marginal rate of return from R & D was 53 percent, Evenson found it was 57 percent, and Schultz found it was 42 percent.[35]

Thus, practically all of the studies carried out to date indicate that the average social rate of return from investments in new technology in both manufacturing and agriculture has tended to be very high. Moreover, the marginal social rate of returns also seems to have been high, generally at least 30 percent. As I have stressed elsewhere,[36] there is a variety of important limitations and problems inherent in each of these studies, and it would be unwise to put too much weight on them. Nonetheless, the fact that so many studies based on quite different techniques and data come to such similar conclusions is impressive.

PUBLIC POLICY ALTERNATIVES

The available evidence, although relevant and interesting, is too weak to indicate with any degree of certainty whether there is an underinvestment in civilian R & D of various sorts.[37] Nonetheless, since the evidence seems to point in this direction, there have been suggestions that tax credits for R & D be adopted, that more federal contracts and grants be used in support of civilian technology, that the government initiate and expand work of the relevant kinds in its own laboratories, that the government insure a portion of private credit to firms for R & D and other innovation costs, that the government use its own purchasing procedures to encourage technological change in the private sector, and that the government use its regulatory policies to try to encourage R & D in the private sector.

It seems fair to say that most economists who have studied this problem have come away with the impression that a general tax credit for R & D would be a relatively inefficient way of increasing federal support for R & D in the private sector. This is because it would reward many firms for doing what they would have done anyway, and it would be likely to encourage the same sorts of R & D that are already being done. Further, it would be an invitation to firms to redefine various activities as R & D. A tax credit for *increases* in R & D spending would be less objectionable on these grounds, but it too is frequently regarded as inefficient because it is not sufficiently selective, and it too runs into the problem that firms could redefine R & D. To get the most impact from a certain level of federal support, it seems to be generally agreed that a more selective technique would be desirable.

However, to utilize more selective techniques, some way must be found to determine where the social payoff from additional federal support is greater (or at least relatively high). The way that most economists would approach this problem is to use some form of benefit-cost analysis to evaluate the payoff from additional federal support of various kinds of R & D. Unfortunately, although such methods are of some use, they are not able to provide very dependable guidance as to how additional federal support for civilian technology should be allocated, due in large part to the fact that the benefits and costs from various kinds of R & D are very hard to forecast.[38] Thus, the choice between the general and more selective forms of support is not as simple as it may seem at first. And when one recognizes that the estimates constructed to guide the selective forms of support may be biased for parochial, selfish, or political reasons, the choice becomes even more difficult.[39] Because of these and other problems, economists have tended to be rather cautious in their recommendations.

Nonetheless, there seem to be at least five important points on which there is considerable agreement. First, to the extent that such a program were selective, it should be neither large scale nor organized on a crash basis. Instead, it should be characterized by flexibility, small-scale probes, and parallel approaches. In view of the relatively small amount of information that is available and the great uncertainties involved, it should be organized, at least in part, to provide information concerning the returns from a larger program. On the basis of the information that results, a more informed judgment could be made concerning the desirability of increased or—for that matter—perhaps decreased amounts of support.

Second, the frequent temptation to focus the program on economically beleaguered industries should be rejected. The fact that an industry is in trouble, or that it is declining, or that it has difficulty competing with foreign firms is, by itself, no justification for additional R & D. More R & D may not have much payoff in such circumstances, or even if it does, the additional resources may have a bigger payoff somewhere else in the economy.

Third, most economists who specialize in this area seem to believe that, except in the most unusual circumstances, the government should avoid getting involved in the latter stages of development work. In general, this seems to be an area where firms are more adept than government agencies. As Keith Pavitt has put it, government programs in support of civilian technology "should be managed on an incremental, step-by-step basis, with the purpose of reducing key scientific and technical uncertainties to a degree that private firms can use the resulting knowledge to decide when (with their own money) they should move into full-scale commercial development."[40]

Fourth, in any selective government program to increase support for civilian technology, it is vitally important that a proper coupling occur between technology and the market. Recent studies of industrial innovations point repeatedly to the key importance of this coupling.[41]

Fifth, most economists seem to be impressed by the advantages in this area of pluralism and decentralized decision-making. Technological change, particularly of a major or radical sort, is marked by great uncertainty. It is difficult to predict which of a number of alternative projects will turn out best. Very important concepts and ideas come from unexpected sources. Consequently, there seems to be a widespread feeling that it would be a mistake for a program of this sort to rely too heavily on centralized direction.

TECHNOLOGICAL FORECASTING

What can be said about the future rate of technological change in the United States? Will technology advance at about the same rate in the next thirty years as it has in the last thirty years, thus promoting a potential rate of economic growth equal to that in the postwar period? Or will it advance less rapidly, thus dragging down the potential rate of economic growth? In recent years, there has been a spectacular increase in the amount of attention devoted by social scientists, management scientists, and others to technological forecasting. New journals on this subject have appeared, and firms and research groups specializing in this subject have come into being. What tools have the technological forecasters developed to help us answer questions of this sort?

According to various surveys, as well as the leading texts on technological forecasting, simple intuitive projections seem to play a very important role in this field.[42] In other words, to forecast the course of technology, one simply asks an expert, or group of experts, to guess as best they can what course it will take. Certainly, this approach is straightforward and relatively cheap. But it runs into a number of difficulties. First, technologists are no more in agreement about the future than are economists, with the result that the forecast is likely to vary, depending on the expert. Second, even when based on the opinion of the most distinguished experts, such forecasts can contain large errors: for example, Vannevar Bush predicted in 1945 that a 3,000 mile rocket would be impossible for many years.[43]

To deal with some of the problems involved in simply asking a group of experts for a consensus guess, O. Helmer and T. Gordon, then at the RAND Corporation, formulated a technique known as the Delphi method, which attempts to utilize expert opinion more effectively.[44] According to this method, one asks a number of experts to formulate separate and independent forecasts. Then the median and interquartile range of the forecasts would be communicated to each of the experts, and they would be asked to reconsider their previous answers and revise them if they desired. Those people whose answers lie outside the interquartile range would be asked to state why they disagree to this extent from other members of the group. Their replies would be circulated among the group, and the members would be asked once again to make a forecast. This iterative process would continue until there was a reasonable convergence of the individual forecasts.

It is important to recognize the obvious fact that the results of the Delphi method can be no better than the foresight of the individual experts. And, as noted above, this foresight can be rather blurred. Moreover by relying so heavily on a consensus, the Delphi method assumes that collective judgment is better than individual judgment. This is a hazardous assumption, as evidenced by the many technological advances that have been made by people who acted contrary to prevailing majority (and elite) opinion.

Another technique that plays an important role in technological forecasting is simple trend extrapolation. In other words, to forecast the rate of technological advance, one extrapolates, as best one can, the rate of technological advance in the past. The problem with such extrapolation is that, unless the fundamental factors determining the rate of technological change operate much as they have in the past, previous trends will not necessarily be a good guide to the future.

Still other techniques that have begun to be used in technological forecasting are input-output models and diffusion models.[45] These techniques seem somewhat more sophisticated than those described above. Unfortunately however, they are still in their infancy, and it is by no means obvious how they could be used to make reasonably accurate forecasts of the rate of technological change in the next thirty years.

To sum up, it appears that the literature on technological forecasting is unlikely to help us forecast the rate of technological advance in the United States in the next thirty years. Most of the techniques commonly used for technological forecasting seem crude, even by the standards of the social and management sciences. In view of this crudeness, it seems unlikely that the results can be at all accurate. But as matters stand, one cannot even be sure of this, since there have been no studies measuring the track record of various kinds of technological forecasting techniques.

CONCLUSIONS

To forecast the rate of technological change, we would like to have a model that shows the relationship between the rate of technological change and the various factors that help to determine this rate. It is clear that the rate of technological change depends on a host of variables, such as the amount spent on R & D by industry, government, and not-for-profit organizations (including universities), the amount of effort put forth by independent inventors, the extent of "learning by doing," the rate of advance of basic science, the quality of our educational system, the extent to which talented young people are attracted by science and engineering, the attitude of the public toward science and technology, and the nature of the government's policies toward full employment, inflation, taxes, patents, and competition. Clearly, no model is available which shows the relationship between all of these variables and the rate of technological change. Nor is such a model likely to be constructed in the near future.

Even if we had such a model, it would be necessary to forecast what government policies and public attitudes will be in years to come in order to plug these exogenous variables into the model. For example, as pointed out above, there is pressure is some quarters for more government support of civilian technology. If such a program were well designed, it might have a significant positive effect on our rate of technological change; whereas if it were poorly designed, it could have a negative effect. At present, there is no way to tell what sort of program, if any, will be adopted in the next thirty years. Similarly, the rate of technological change will depend on the public's attitudes toward the risks involved in pushing technology forward. And there is no way to forecast these attitudes either.

In the absence of a satisfactory model or of a way to forecast many of the exogenous variables, any attempt to forecast the rate of technological change is obviously hazardous. Nonetheless, it seems most unlikely that technological change will no longer contribute to economic growth. As we have seen, it has played a very major role in the promotion of economic growth in the past seventy years (and more). There is no reason to think that it will no longer do so in the future. Given the large expenditures on R & D, as well as the efforts of independent inventors and others, one would expect that a stream of new products and processes, as well as product and process improvements, will continue to lighten mankind's burden and increase his (or her) well-being.

Although it is very difficult to predict the kinds of advances that will be made, it seems likely that progress will be made in areas like energy where very large sums are being devoted to R & D. For example, efforts are currently being made to convert our relatively plentiful coal supplies into a clean gas or other forms of fuel that would be less polluting than coal. The federal government has helped to finance several approaches to coal gasification, such as the Institute of Gas Technology's HYGAS pilot plant, the Consolidation Coal Company's CO_2 Acceptor pilot plant, FMC Corporation's COED pilot plant, and others. The United States has over 300 billion tons of coal reserves, more than any other country in the world. It seems probable that improved ways will be found eventually to utilize this vast treasure.

Important advances may also occur in many other areas. For example, it was announced recently that scientists have used recombinant-DNA technology and artificial gene synthesis to produce a brain hormone. Since there is considerable worry about recombinant-DNA research and its potential for harm, this example illustrates the problems in assessing new technology as well. The National Institutes of Health, which have funded many recombinant-DNA research programs, have issued guidelines to promote the safety of such experiments.

Whereas it seems likely that technological change will continue to promote economic growth throughout the world, there is more question concerning whether or not the rate of technological change in the U.S. will be as great as in the past. Some observers seem to feel that unless corrective action is taken the rate of technological change in the United States may decline (at least, relative to other countries, if not in absolute terms). For example, Robert Gilpin and Charles Kindleberger, among others, have discussed some of the factors pointing in that direction: the slackening of U.S. productivity growth, the reduced share of GNP going for R & D, and the apparent narrowing of the U.S. technological lead over other countries.[46] However, as policymakers recognize, indicators of this sort are very imperfect guides to the present, let alone to the future. As pointed out above, the slackening of U.S. productivity growth may be due in large part to a variety of factors other than a reduction in the rate of technological change; the reduction in the share of GNP going for R & D, due primarily to a reduction in space and defense R & D, may not have such a great impact on civilian technology; and the narrowing of the U.S. technological lead may be largely an expected reflection of Germany's and Japan's getting back on their feet after the war. Thus, just as many of the dire warnings concerning the effects of the technology gap issued only 15 years ago seem out of tune with the current scene, so many of the present warnings concerning our rate of technological change may seem exaggerated when viewed with the benefit of hindsight. On the other hand, however, there is no assurance that the slowdown will not occur. Thus, it would be irresponsible and foolish to ignore the current warnings.

Nonetheless, given the current uncertainties, as well as the enormous difficulties involved in peering into the murky future, it seems to me that we should be careful not to overreact. This is so since we know so little about the ways in which public policy can be used effectively to promote a more rapid rate of technological change in civilian areas. What is perhaps most important at present is that sound research be carried out by economists, scientists, engineers, and research administrators to indicate more clearly how public policy can be used effectively to influence the rate and direction of technological change.[47] If, as time goes on, it becomes clearer that our rate of technological change is declining—and that we as a nation want to increase it—we shall need a much better understanding of these matters than is currently available. Without such improved understanding, even if it becomes much clearer that we want to try to stimulate civilian technology, we may have to depend on a very limited and unsatisfactory set of policy tools.

NOTES

[1.] Moses Abramowitz, "Rapid Growth Potential and Its Realization: The Experience of Capitalist Economies in the Postwar Period" (Paper presented at the Fifth World Congress of the International Economic Association, August 1977), p.4. Note that this paper is not concerned only with the United States.

2. Robert Solow, "Technical Change and the Aggregate Production Function," *Review of Economics and Statistics*, August 1957.

3. Edward Denison, *The Sources of Economic Growth in the United States* (New York: Committee for Economic Development, 1962).

4. Moses Abramowitz, "Resources and Output Trends in the United States since 1870," *American Economic Review*, May 1956; and Solomon Fabricant, "Economic Progress and Economic Change," 34th Annual Report of the National Bureau of Economic Research (New York, 1954).

5. Jorg Minasian, "Research and Development, Production Functions, and Rates of Return," *American Economic Review*, May 1969.

6. Edwin Mansfield, *Industrial Research and Technological Innovation* (New York: W. W. Norton/Cowles Foundation, 1968).

7. Zvi Griliches, "Returns to Research and Development in the Private Sector" (New York: National Bureau of Economic Research, Conference on Research in Income and Wealth, 1975); M. Ishaq Nadiri and Georges Bitros, "Research and Development Expenditures and Labor Productivity at the Firm Level," *Ibid.;* and Nestor Terleckyj, *Effects of R & D on the Productivity Growth of Industries; An Exploratory Study* (Washington, D.C.: National Planning Association, 1974).

8. John Enos, *Petroleum Progress and Profits* (Cambridge, Mass.: M.I.T. Press, 1962), and J. Tilton, *International Diffusion of Technology: The Case of Semiconductors* (Washington, D.C.: Brookings, 1971).

9. Edwin Mansfield, "Contribution of R & D to Economic Growth in the United States," *Science*, 4 February 1972.

10. Ronald Kutscher, Jerome Mark, and John Norsworthy, "The Productivity Slowdown and the Outlook to 1985," *Monthly Labor Review*, May 1977.

11. These figures come from John Kendrick, "Productivity Trends and Prospects," in *U.S. Economic Growth from 1976 to 1986* (Washington, D.C.: Joint Economic Committee of Congress, 1 October 1976), vol. 1, p.19.

12. Kutscher, Mark, and Norsworthy, *"Productivity Slowdown."*

13. Edward Denison, *Accounting for United States Economic Growth, 1929-69* (Washington, D.C.: Brookings, 1974); and George Perry, "Labor Structure, Potential Output, and Productivity," in *Brookings Papers on Economic Activity* (Washington, D.C.: Brookings, 1971).

14. Laurits Christensen, Dianne Cummings, and Dale Jorgensen, "An International Comparison of Growth of Productivity, 1947-73" (New York: National Bureau of Economic Research, Conference on Research in Income and Wealth, 1975).

15. William Nordhaus, "The Recent Productivity Slowdown," in *Brookings Papers on Economic Activity* (Washington, D.C.: Brookings, 1972).

16. Michael Grossman and Victor Fuchs, "Intersectoral Shifts and Aggregate Productivity Change," *Annals of Economic and Social Measurement* (New York: National Bureau of Economic Research, 1973); and Kutscher, Mark, and Norsworthy, "Productivity Slowdown."

17. Kendrick, "Productivity Trends and Prospects."

18. For a discussion of these spillover effects, see Edwin Mansfield, *The Economics of Technological Change* (New York: Norton, 1968).

19. See Edwin Manfield, John Rapoport, Anthony Romeo, Edmond Villani, Samuel Wagner, and Frank Husic, *The Production and Application of New Industrial Technology* (New York: Norton, 1977).

20. U.S. Department of Commerce, *U.S. Technology Policy: A Draft Study* (Washington, D.C.: National Technical Information Service (PB-263 806), March 1977). Note that, although R & D spending often is expressed as a percent of GNP, there is no reason to believe that it is sound public policy to maintain this percentage at a particular level. More will be said below on this score.

21. Edwin Mansfield, "Technology and Technological Change," in John Dunning, *Economic Analysis and the Multinational Enterprise* (London: George Allen and Unwin, 1974).

22. *Gaps in Technology: General Report* (Paris: Organization for Economic Cooperation and Development, 1968).

23. For example, see Robert Gilpin, *Technology, Economic Growth, and Economic Competitiveness* (Washington, D.C.: Joint Economic Committee of Congress, 9 July 1975).

24. Christensen, Cummings, and Jorgensen "Comparison of Growth of Productivity."

25. See *Science Indicators, 1974* (Washington, D.C.: National Science Foundaton, 1975).

26. However, it should be noted that the United States devotes a much larger proportion of its R & D expenditures to defense and space than do France, West Germany, the United Kingdom, or Japan.

27. For example, see William Fellner, "The Progress-Generating Sector's Claim to High Priority," *Research and Development and Economic Growth/Productivity* (Washington, D.C.: National Science Foundation, 1971) and Richard Nelson, Merton Peck, and Edward Kalachek, *Technology, Economic Growth, and Public Policy* (Washington, D.C.: Brookings, 1967).

28. For further discussion, see Edwin Mansfield, "Federal Support of R and D Activities in the Private Sector," *Priorities and Efficiency in Federal Research and Develop-*

ment (Washington, D.C.: Joint Economic Committee of Congress, October 29, 1976).

29. For a description of these techniques, see the works cited in notes 30 and 31.

30. Zvi Griliches, "Research Costs and Social Returns: Hybrid Corn and Related Innovations," *Journal of Political Economy*, October 1958; Willis Peterson, "The Returns to Investment in Agricultural Research in the United States," in *Resource Allocation in Agricultural Research* (St. Paul: University of Minnesota, 1971); and Andrew Schmitz and David Seckler, "Mechanized Agriculture and Social Welfare: The Case of the Tomato Harvester," *American Journal of Agricultural Economics*, 1970.

31. Edwin Mansfield, John Rapoport, Anthony Romeo, Samuel Wagner, and George Beardsley, "Social and Private Rates of Return from Industrial Innovations," *Quarterly Journal of Economics*, May 1977.

32. Edwin Mansfield, *et al., Production and Application of New Industrial Technology.*

33. Mansfield, *Industrial Research and Technological Innovation.*

34. Minasian, "Research and Development."

35. Zvi Griliches, "Research Expenditures, Education, and the Aggregate Production Function," *American Economic Review*, December 1964; Robert Evenson, "The Contribution of Agricultural Research and Extension to Agricultural Production" (Ph.D. thesis, University of Chicago, 1968); and Theodore Schultz, *The Economic Organization of Agriculture* (New York: McGraw-Hill, 1953).

36. See Mansfield, "Contribution of R and D."

37. In this section, I have borrowed freely from my paper cited in note 28, as well as from the paper I presented to the Fifth World Congress of the International Economic Association on 31 August 1977 and the paper I gave at the National Science Foundation on 9 November 1977.

38. Recent studies indicate that it is difficult indeed to forecast the R & D costs required to produce a given capability, and that major corporations have problems in using various forms of benefit-cost analysis for R & D project selection, even though they have a much easier benefit concept to estimate than most government agencies do. See George Beardsley and Edwin Mansfield, "A Note on the Accuracy of Industrial Forecasts of the Profitability of New Products and Processes," *Journal of Business*, January 1978; and Edwin Mansfield, John Rapoport, Jerome Schnee, Samuel Wagner, and Michael Hamburger, *Research and Innovation in the Modern Corporation* (New York: Norton, 1971).

39. George Eads, "U.S. Government Support for Civilian Technology: Economic Theory vs. Political Practice," *Research Policy*, 1974.

40. Keith Pavitt, "A Survey of the Literature on Government Policy Towards Innovation," unpublished, 1975.

41. See Christopher Freeman, *The Economics of Industrial Innovation* (London: Penguin, 1974) and the books cited in notes 19 and 38.

42. Among the most prominent texts on this subject are Erich Jantsch, *Technological Forecasting in Perspective* (Paris: Organization for Economic Cooperation and Development, 1967); James Bright, *Technological Forecasting for Industry and Government* (Englewood Cliffs, N.J.: Prentice Hall, 1968); Marvin Cetron, *Technological Forecasting: A Practical Approach* (New York: Gordon and Breach, 1969); and Robert Ayres, *Technological Forecasting and Long-Range Planning* (New York: McGraw-Hill, 1969).

43. For other examples, see Mansfield, "The Economics of Technological Change."

44. See Theodore Gordon and Olaf Helmer, *Report on a Long-Range Forecasting Study*, RAND Corporation Report P-2982, September 1964, as well as the articles by Helmer and Gordon in Bright, *Technological Forecasting.*

45. See Edwin Mansfield, "Technological Forecasting," in T. Khachaturov, *Methods of Long-Term Planning and Forecasting* (London, Macmillan, 1976).

46. See Robert Gilpin, *Technology, Economic Growth;* and Charles Kindleberger, "An American Economic Climacteric?" *Challenge,* January 1974. In considerable part, these authors are concerned about our rate of technological change, relative to that of other nations.

47. I do not mean to imply that research of this kind is not going on. The National Science Foundation is financing and conducting a considerable amount of such work. What I'm trying to stress is the importance of research of this sort.

THREE

The Role of Capital Creation

Norma Pace
Senior Vice President
American Paper Institute

INTRODUCTION

Capital formation has been called the nation's third-century challenge. This top billing reflects the relatively slow recovery in plant and equipment spending from the 1974-75 recession. When coupled with the memory of serious shortages in many basic materials that prevailed in 1973 and early 1974, this lag in new investment in facilities looms as a major threat to job formation, cost-price inflation, the free market system, and indeed the political stability of the world.

With the world's population growing at a 2 percent per year rate, the 4 billion inhabitants of this planet will double to 8 billion in thirty-five years. Furthermore, it has been estimated that if current per capita rates of consumption were to continue to advance without change, the average person's claim on the world's resources, including capital, would double between now and the end of the century. Normally such forecasts of demand would speed up the entrepreneurial search for opportunity and high yields and lead to increased investments. The demand challenges implied by this people flow would fire the creativity and ingenuity of investors and pave the way for a better life for all; in short, it would act to stimulate economic growth. The system worked that way during the past, especially during the post-World-War-II period. But now there is serious questioning of the value of economic growth, of the ability of the world's resources to support growth, and even more fundamentally, the need for growth.

Multinational corporations, economists, and investors who had been on the traditional growth path suddenly found the road blocked by a series of socio-political and ecological concerns which culminated in the quadrupling of oil prices in 1974 and the grim realization that the finite supply of resources could pose severe restraints to long-term growth. A change in economic orientation seems to be occurring and producers are asked to shift their sights from the satisfaction of created wants to the sharing of limited material resources. Our Free Choice Economy may be turning into a Scarcity Economy. This phenomenon has already impacted capital spending and has led to strong and unpalatable actions for redistributing the nation's wealth and indeed the wealth of the world.

The current lag in capital spending gives recognition to the possibility that the structure of the industrial world's economies may be changing; this creates doubts about the need for physical additions to the capital stock. When in doubt, businessmen and the investors wait it out on a more secure island of cash and government securities. The holdings of cash and U.S. government securities minus federal income tax liabilities has grown from $51 billion at the end of 1974 to $78 billion in mid-1977.[1] Liquidity is not the problem, but confidence is. The investment decisions which normally incorporate a certain amount of risk, cannot be reconciled easily with the new dimensions that have been added, such as higher energy cost and availability, price inflation, worldwide stagnation, and the absorption of costly environmental and safety outlays.

These concerns with growth have not gone unnoticed in Washington where policymakers have been debating the question of growth, full employment, and inflation under the new structural constraints. A new version of the Humphrey-Hawkins bill establishing growth and full employment goals is now moving through the congressional procedures. The lag in capital formation is occurring at an inconvenient time when the number of entrants into the labor force is at an all time high. This labor force pressure will continue until the mid-1980s, after which labor force growth will begin to moderate. At least 2.5 million new jobs a year will have to be created during the next decade.

How can the U.S. society organize itself to employ these human resources fully? Does it need a proportionate increase in the capital stock? Does it need more capital spending and, if so, where?

Some signals on the plant and equipment spending needs of the next decade are clear but many remain fuzzy. Investments in all forms of energy will be large, including outlays to increase efficiency and reduce BTU input, along with investments in new supply. Environmentally related outlays will continue to expand and outlays associated with science and technology—particularly computer related technology—also will multiply rapidly.

The uncertain areas center around basic industries, such as steel, textiles, paper, metalworking, et cetera. What is their role in the growth scenarios of the next ten to fifteen years? Should the country induce capital formation in industries such as these which have the common characteristic of being in excess supply in almost all producing countries? And if one needed more negative arguments, one could add that these industries are generally heavy energy users and bear significant antipollution costs.

The matter of capital formation will be debated even more as the Administration and Congress consider the question of how to split the promised tax cut. Should the historical one-third to business and two-thirds to individuals be maintained?

This all important political question is beyond the understanding of the average citizen. Workers continue to demand increases in their standard of living and their concerns are primarily with their job security, their pay, and family needs and wants. They know little about how these needs are met and particularly about the contribution of capital. Ask the man on the street about capital formation and you will get a cold stare. How then can we talk about having a major challenge in capital formation without general understanding and general acceptance of the problem? Where can the average intelligent interested American find out about capital formation? My experience tells me it is a well-kept secret. Of all the jargon in economics, capital formation stands out as one of the more unfortunate expressions.

Obviously, the question of capital formation and its relationship to growth suffers from gross neglect in schools, media, and cocktail parties. Full employment, on the other hand, is an exciting topic, easy to understand and to talk about. Credit for its popularizaton must be given to the Employment Act of 1946 and the dedicated efforts of our public servants to implement that act.

So the first lesson to learn from the post-World-War-II "New" and

"New New" Economics is that we must find another name for this vital link between jobs, people, freedom, and independence, and we must popularize it.

This analysis deals with several important questions:

What is capital formation? How much capital formation is needed? Does capital investment help job formation? Is capital investment changing because of the altered structure of the economy? Does capital formation help productivity and will lack of capital formation create shortages? Considering the world's excess capacity in some basic industries should capital formation be encouraged? Have taxing policies affected capital formation?

What Is Capital Formation?

Capital formation is the process of channeling investment into productive facilities. But what are productive facilities? Plant and equipment immediately come to mind but should we include investment in highways, education, and housing as well? One could have an endless debate over what constitutes capital formation; many tables which show an unfavorable comparison between U.S. investment and that of other countries actually include the broader definition.

A more precise comparison of the U.S. share of Gross National Product (GNP) going into plant and equipment with that of other major countries shows the U.S. is not far behind.

Our problem is not one of lagging investment vis-à-vis other countries but rather insufficient investment to meet the full employment needs of the U.S. economy.

My definition of capital formation will be confined to one of channelizing investment into plant and equipment.

How Much Capital Formation?

The United States allocated 10.5 percent of its real gross national expenditures to investment in plant and equipment during the 1965-75 period. Other industrial countries range higher and lower as is shown below:

Japan	17.6%
Germany	15.3

Italy	6.8
France	12.9
United Kingdom	9.3

In the less industrialized countries, the share tends to be lower as the following figures for 1970-76 for Australia and Brazil indicate:

| Australia | 7.8% |
| Brazil | 4.0 |

Several conclusions are obvious from these data. High investment countries have high employment and high standards of living. The reverse is true for low investment countries. We know that an investment of 3-4 percent of GNP in plant and equipment is probably too low, but 15-20 percent could be too high. Certainly in the capital goods boom periods of 1955-57 and 1965-69 in the United States, the levels were too high and were followed by significant contractions in investment in plant and equipment with accompanying reductions in employment. There is no doubt that new investment in plant and equipment must advance more rapidly in the years ahead but in our anxiety to correct for the deficient level of investment in productive facilities in recent years, let us make certain that we do not produce the reverse situations of overinvestment and oversaving. That too, would have devastating consequences.

What is lacking in the system is a mechanism that smoothly balances savings and investment outlays with consumption requirements. In the past, that adjustment was painfully made by sharp cycles in investment; two or three years of high investment were followed by a few years of low capital formation. Without the proper adjusting mechanism for investment, unstable economc conditions result, accompanied by inflation and layoffs.

Over the years society has been striving to find that balancing mechanism. The Employment Act of 1946 was intended to help correct the severe adjustments in the economy that were required after a bout of heavy savings and investment. But that mechanism did not perform a balancing function; over time it was politicized into one that encourages undersaving and overspending. The Employment Act and other efforts to redistribute income, such as the Great Society programs of the 1960s, have combined to channel more savings into government debt and less into plant and equipment. Taxes and federal budgetary deficits were the means for effecting this shift but conventional banking practices also contribute to the change. Taxes are imposed on savings and the return on savings; they are imposed on both the investment and the return on investment. The double taxation on savings and investment is no longer borne by the rich alone; it has hit middle-class America as inflation pushes more and more wage earners up the progressive tax rate scale and into the double tax penalty on savings.

The banking system, too, has a quirk in its semantics—when banks lend money to corporations, that transaction is called *loans,* but when they lend money to the federal government, that transaction is labeled *investment.* The ratio of loans to investments is one measure of the quality or liquidity of a bank's portfolio; the higher the ratio, the riskier the assets. This evaluation flows from the taxing power of the federal government, which always makes it creditworthy—and presumably able to repay its debt. Thus, as banks reach out for a wide variety of loans, such as consumer installment and real estate loans, they have to curtail loans for production facilities in order to maintain reasonable risk ratios. The 1973 money "crunch" saw some of this process of unhealthy diversion from investment in production facilities to other outlets. The problem at that time was not only a shortage of money encouraged by Federal Reserve policies, but also the quality of its distribution among borrowers.

It is time to reevaluate standard measurements of performance in bank portfolios to prevent shifts that penalize productive investments. I stress this point because the banking system through its power over the cost and availability of money has historically been the major stopgap to a surge in capital spending. Can it perform that function in a timely way? The past record of performance is most discouraging and the problem is even more difficult now. The outlets for funds are very varied and the direct control of the Federal Reserve is shrinking.

Furthermore, Federal Reserve policy in the past has never adequately taken into account changes in the velocity of spending or the rate of use of money. More recently Chairman Burns of the Federal Reserve has called attention to the importance of this factor in money transactions, although he admits that velocity is difficult to anticipate.

In the past, Federal Reserve policy was geared to reports on loans to business. Excessive lending signaled the Fed that bank lending had to be curtailed through restricted availability and higher costs. What the past policy failed to recognize is that heavy loan demand is a lagging indicator; it generally describes the end of an investment spending spree, not the beginning. At the time the Federal Reserve was tightening money to prevent excessive borrowing, it should have been worrying about the downtrend in velocity that would occur as many corporations completed their capital programs and reduced their demands for labor in capital goods industries.

While this lag is now recognized, the management of monetary policy still suffers from the high degree of personal judgment and discretion used in decision making. It will never be different under the present mechanism but substituting more government control over bank lending policies will do more harm than good. We need to evolve a money system that works mechanically, neither overrewarding, nor overpenalizing savers and investors. Chairman Burns is to be commended for reintroducing velocity into discussions of appropriate money policy but until monetary policy is better attuned, the Federal government will have more and more involvement in spending decisions.

The question of how much plant and equipment spending is required will never be answered in precise terms. What is needed is a mechanism that moderates periods of both under- and oversaving. To put it another way, orderly growth requires a stable velocity in spending decisions; yet the ever growing presence of government during the past decade has had the opposite effect on investment decisions. Additions to the capital stock have lagged behind additions to the labor force since 1970. Forecasts of capital stock requirements in the decade ahead suggest that the U.S. economy must allocate at least one percent more of its GNP to business investment, that is, 11.5 percent to 12 percent. Energy, environment, and efficiency call for this higher allocation. This recognition alone is forcing the government to take positive tax actions to help finance these additional outlays.

CAPITAL INVESTMENT AND JOBS

Aside from the correlation implied by the fact that countries with high investment are countries with generally high employment, there is the specific question of how capital formation affects jobs in specific industries and locations.

To the average person a new machine can mean a displaced worker; labor unions have a long history of fighting productivity changes and investments in the mistaken belief that investment causes unemployment. For the displaced workers the concern is a real one. For the union, which is losing membership and dues, the concern is understandable. But for the nation as a whole, the problem need not be a problem. Heavy investment in plant and equipment which reduces the input of labor per unit of output, transfers jobs from one plant to another and most likely from one city to another. Capital spending creates jobs for architects, engineers, and workers in machinery plants, all of whom are receiving income from the savings of the nation. These earnings increase the demand for consumer goods, resulting in increased operating rates in those industries and further advances in capital goods spending. The multiplier effect of a capital goods dollar in the system is proven to be large.

The plight of displaced workers is the problem. They will have to find new jobs and may need new skills; this type of adjustment is possible but is not pleasant: For the worker who is sixty-two years old, it may not even be possible. Success requires mobility of labor, training schools, and a commitment by employers to help the disemployed. Personnel management must incorporate this dimension in its activities. Happily, help with such painful adjustment is increasingly a part of standard procedures for employers. (This plant-by-plant adjustment for workers displaced by technology, is in contrast with the large scale layoffs required by a nationwide contraction in economic activity.)

Increased emphasis on research and development is a natural accompaniment to this process of job shift for such investments will create the new industries and jobs for displaced workers.

A friend gave me a wonderful title for this: he calls it "intellectual capital formation." In the mid-1960s when we were excited about putting a man on the moon the rate of intellectual capital formation was high. Computer technology was advanced; miniaturization increased; the nation's technology is still feeding off of that glowing input. Our intellectual energies since then have been dissipated while Europeans and the Japanese seem to be running faster. We need to restore a cli-

mate that permits intellectual capital formation to flourish and this requires the coordinated attention of university research activities, business, and government.

Pension plans must recognize the impact of the greater need for
mobility in the labor force. Although many employers are concerned
over the high funding requirements of portability of pension plans, it
seems fair that if employers are given the privilege to terminate
employment in the name of technology and efficiency, they also have a
responsibility to give displaced workers the portion of the pension that
accrues for time invested in the company.

Some analysts claim that capital formation increases the demand for
skilled workers alone and bypasses the problem of the large pool of
available unskilled workers. This conclusion seems to be based upon
recent performance in the capital goods and labor markets, a performance that has been distorted by destabilizing government policies, and
by an unusual flow of teenagers and women into the labor force. At the
early stages of an advance in capital goods spending the demand for
skilled workers does rise and these are absorbed first. But eventually
capital goods producers have to expand training programs to develop
the skills needed. Long-range planning of most businesses incorpor-
ates future personnel requirements and the use of training programs to
achieve the desired size and quality of the firm's future labor force.

The unemployment rate today belies the shortages of skilled workers. Want ads for skilled workers remain large. At present there is no
large pool of skilled labor available; the unemployment rate for experienced wage and salary workers of 6.6 percent is only 2 percent above
the 1974 low and provides only a small growth potential. Further increases in the demand for capital goods will encourage the training of
individuals with marginal skills. So long as the plant capacity to expand output exists, managers will seek to train workers to meet the
higher demand for their goods.

Expansion in capital spending will not solve the problem of the so-
called unemployables; that is a cost society must bear directly through
income assistance and enlightened welfare programs. The error in
policy actions during the past ten years has been the trade-off of investment in new job creating facilities for direct government spending
to help the poor. Inflation was the result and this helped no one.
Growth in real output provides the only real means for helping the

poor. Goods and services are what they need and not dollars.

Recently I had occasion to study the income distribution of the U.S. in real terms from 1960 to date. The picture is remarkable; progress in reducing the number earning under $3000 a year and in increasing the number earning over $15,000 in real terms was good until 1969. After 1969 progress slowed and was finally halted. Inflation was taking its toll across the board. Not only did real growth slow down between 1968 and 1976 but the improvement in its distribution came to a grinding stop. Income figures alone do not convey the whole story about the distribution of goods and services. But it is impressive to note that federal budget deficits aggregated $296 billion, between 1969 and 1977, deficits that were generated by rapidly rising help-the-poor programs of the federal government. This spending did little to improve the real wealth of its citizens, especially low-income citizens.

CAPITAL FORMATION AND THE STRUCTURE OF THE ECONOMY

Service industries have become the major employees of the nation's labor force. Just thirty years ago the number of people producing goods (employees in manufacturing, construction, and farming) matched the number involved in services. Now the number of service employees is 2.4 times the number of employees in goods-producing industries. This has both a cause and effect impact on capital formation.

The introduction of labor-saving equipment on farms, in the factory, and in construction has reduced the manpower input for goods production; but it also helped finance the increase in services which became a necessary part of a growing standard of living and it released the manpower to provide these services. But service industries are not supposed to generate as much investment requirements as goods industries. While this may be true in terms of dollars of new investment per dollar of output, the investment needs generated by the service industries are nonetheless large. It is easily recognized that the equipment needs of the telephone, utility, and transportation industries run into billions of dollars per year. However, fast food chains, wholesale and retail operations, et cetera also spend a great deal for new stores, special equipment, trucks, and computer installations. Note, too, the heavy investments of the securities industry in computer and communication equipment. The products bought for investment by the service industries may be different than for goods production but the total number of dollars is significant. Thus, the continuing shift in employment from goods-producing industries to services will redirect and not lessen investment requirements.

The figures on plant and equipment expenditures by major industries show that outlays by manufacturing firms in 1977 at $60.6 billion will be 32 percent above 1974 levels, only a shade ahead of the inflation rate for capital goods. In nonmanufacturing industries the advance was only 14 percent during that period.[2] The shortfall seems to be in this sector of the economy, and there is good reason for this. Public utility outlays are lagging needs primarily because of environmental concerns. Nuclear power plant construction has been delayed by the concerns of environmentalists; coal consumption has been reduced because of air quality problems. Utilities began to increase outlays significantly in 1977 in response to the pressures of the energy crisis. In other nonmanufacturing industries, pressures for increasing capital spending are developing from the large increase in the number of people in the active spending and consuming ages.

The largest growth industry among the service groups, insofar as employment is concerned, is the federal government. Investments in new communication equipment will probably accelerate in the future so that capital investment in this high labor content industry should advance also.

Finally, state and local governments will increase their investments in schools, highways, waterworks, and other services and thereby increase the demand for other productive investments.

So the changing structure of the U.S. economy not only depends upon rising capital formation—but it also feeds the demand for capital as well.

CAPITAL FORMATION, PRODUCTIVITY, AND INFLATION

Productivity is commonly measured by calculating output per manhour. While economists have been striving to measure productivity in terms of a broader definition of inputs, including capital and the education of workers as well as the number of manhours, these more erudite measurements are cumbersome and not readily updated. The U.S. Bureau of Labor Statistics data on output per manhour has the merit of being easy to compute and available on a quarterly basis. So long as one recognizes its limitations, the series can be useful.

Table 3.1 compares output per manhour in twelve countries by five-year periods from 1960 to 1975.

These data reflect the combination of output, labor inputs, and the varying reliance on hours of work. Except for the United States, Canada, Japan, and France where hours worked rose, all other countries increased efficiencies by reducing hours. To put it another way, productivity in North America and Japan was dampened by the larger manhour input, reflecting the special structural situations in these economies.

Table 3.1   Output per Hour in Manufacturing: Average Annual Rates of Change, 12 Countries, 5-Year Periods, 1960-75

	(percent)			
Country	1960-75	1960-65	1965-70	1970-75
United States	2.7	4.9	1.4	1.8
Canada	4.0	4.5	4.5	2.7
Japan	9.7	8.5	13.4	5.4
Belgium	7.0	4.8	8.0	7.6
Denmark	7.2	5.4	8.7	6.8
France	5.6	5.2	6.7	3.4
Germany	5.7	6.4	5.6	5.4
Italy	6.2	6.8	5.3	6.0
Netherlands	7.1	5.0	8.7	5.8
Sweden	6.6	7.1	7.6	5.0
Switzerland	5.1	2.3	6.7	3.5
United Kingdom	3.8	4.1	3.7	3.1

SOURCE: "Comparative Growth in Manufacturing Productivity and Labor Costs in Selected Industrialized Countries," *Bulletin No. 1958* (Washington, D.C.: U.S. Department of Labor, Bureau of Labor Statistics, January 1977), p. 6.

NOTE: The percent changes are computed from the least squares trend of the logarithms of the index numbers.

The figures show a reduced trend of productivity in the United States and Japan over time. European countries have managed to maintain a more consistent performance over the fifteen-year period. Obviously future growth trends in output will provide the major thrust to the advance in productivity, but capital will nonetheless contribute significantly to that growth. The production of capital goods is an important element in the industrial base of all these countries so that aggressive investment will by definition translate into faster growth. But there is another dimension to that: While it is recognized that stronger growth in production will be needed in the five years ahead to meet the expectations of people and to improve productivity over recent experience, there is less agreement over the fact that significant capital input may be needed to sustain that growth.

Because labor accounts for more than 70 percent of the cost of producing final goods and services in the U.S., productivity influences unit labor costs which, in turn, influence prices.

Table 3.2 compares changes in unit labor costs in the same twelve countries in their own units of exchange.

Despite the relatively poor performance in productivity in the United States, wage rate increases have been more moderate than in other countries, and the U.S. is maintaining a fairly favorable labor cost base compared with the internal cost structures of other countries. In the U.S., the problem lies in the level of labor costs, which remain higher than in many other countries because of our industry mix, our historic ability to support these higher levels through growth and capital formation, and the maturity of our economy compared with some of our trading partners.

The United States inflation rate seems to be settling down to the 6 percent indicated by unit labor costs. Smaller wage increases are one way to reduce inflation, increased productivity is another. Yet the Congress in 1977 passed Social Security legislation which will add $227.3 billion to labor costs over the next ten years and inflate prices by 0.5 percent a year. Somehow this added cost must find an offset in productivity if some other sector of the economy is not to be shortchanged.

Historically the benefits of higher productivity were split three ways: they were given to consumers in the form of lower prices, to workers in the form of higher wages, and to stockholders in the form of

Table 3.2   Unit Labor Costs in Manufacturing, Based on National Currency Values: Average Annual Rates of Change, 12 Countries, 1960-75

			(percent)	
Country	1960-75	1960-65	1965-70	1970-75
United States	2.9	−1.3	4.6	6.1
Canada	2.8	− .9	3.0	7.1
Japan	5.4	4.3	1.7	14.5
Belgium	4.2	4.6	1.2	8.7
Denmark	4.6	4.0	3.5	8.1
France	4.5	3.8	2.4	11.4
Germany	4.2	3.0	2.5	7.5
Italy	6.7	6.3	3.8	15.2
Netherlands	5.5	5.9	3.0	9.7
Sweden	4.0	3.0	2.1	8.7
Switzerland	3.8	6.3	.4	8.2
United Kingdom	5.7	2.2	3.7	12.9

SOURCE: "Comparative Growth in Manufacturing Productivity and Labor Costs in Selected Industrialized Countries," *Bulletin No. 1958* (Washington, D.C.: U.S. Department of Labor, Bureau of Labor Statistics, January 1977), p. 7.

NOTE: The percent changes are computed from the least squares trend of the logarithms of the index numbers.

higher profits and dividends. In today's society not only are the benefits totally absorbed by labor, but wages rise even faster than productivity. Consumers pay for this in higher prices and shareholders in lower profits and dividends. Until wages are once again realigned with productivity, price inflation will persist. Workers have benefited little from the escalating wage increases. Inflation and the progressive tax system of the nation have drained most of the additional wages, putting workers in a constant position of catching up.

A benign acceptance of smaller wage increases by labor is not in the cards. The Consumer Price Index is still 6 percent ahead of 1976 levels; workers would like at least a 2 percent increase in their standard of living indicating a wage rate increase of 8 percent a year.

More reliance must be placed upon increasing productivity. For the individual firm the solution is to restrain the rise in labor costs by increasing investments in equipment. Companies also will hope for higher output to generate cost savings but the answer must lie in a better management of facilities. The individual plant must be made highly efficient at less than maximum rates of operation. As replacement planning and spending proceeds, new concepts of maximized efficiency may be needed. While across-the-board rules cannot be made, plant managers should aim to increase productivity (and profitability) at lower rates of operation than for all out production. A great deal of the volatility in profit margins, savings, and investments would end with such planning. In other words, economies of scale may not be as beneficial as they once were; this change is already apparent in some investments. Shopping centers are smaller. Mass merchandising stores are built with fewer square feet than their predecessors. Modular-type construction is used more frequently so that add-ons can be made when needed. While these techniques are not applicable in all industries, each will search for the most efficient way to handle volatile changes in demand, high cost energy, and environmental constraints.

To neglect this important area of cost savings will result in greater inflation and reduced profit margins. This, in turn, leads to lower levels of investment.

Replacement costs have almost doubled during the past six years, while replacement needs have escalated. If the job of increasing efficiencies in existing plants is to be accomplished, then industry must retain more of its cash flow.

CAPITAL FORMATION, SOCIAL, AND ENVIRONMENTAL GOALS

Increased urbanization, higher consumption rates per person, and increased use of manmade materials have created social and environmental pressures in the system. These pressures must be relieved and someone has to pay for that; that someone is ultimately the final consumer. This has led to more conflicts in the system—conflicts between environmentalists and producers, environmentalists and government, producers and consumers, consumers and government, producers and government. That conflict represents a tremendous amount of wrenching, twisting, and torsion in the system.

Water and air quality, toxics and solid waste management are regulated by the Environmental Protection Agency. The approach used by the agency is to set standards across the nation and timetables for meeting the standards. Nine basic industries are heavily impacted by these regulations, namely, steel, paper, nonferrous metals, petroleum, electric power, chemicals, transportation, plastics and rubber, all of which show sluggish expansion plans. In some segments of these industries, outlays to meet water and air standards amounted to as much as 18-30 percent of their annual capital budgets. This diversion of capital to retrofit existing facilities is clearly a limiting factor to new investment. Now the plant and equipment spending in these nine basic industries must be carefully monitored in terms of their potential for creating bottlenecks to national growth and full employment over the long run. The agonizing problem of these industries has received the attention of Congress and the EPA. The regulatory processes will be reviewed to determine whether environmental regulations can be moderated without sacrificing environmental quality. A period of slower growth in antipollution outlays would free up more cash flow for new investment than would otherwise be available. It will also help reduce inflationary pressures.

Furthermore, these regulations when soundly based and reasonably administered do provide a thrust to new technology. Most of the environmental expenditures to date have been made to retrofit existing facilities but all new plants and mills being built now take into account the need to preserve the quality of the environment as much as possible.

The paper industry is a remarkable example of making pollution abatement technology pay off insofar as is possible. Recovery boilers, which were installed as a result of the environmental regulations, recapture liquids which can be reused and are an important source of fuel for the industry. Chemicals are also recovered which can be reused or sold. Replacement of old boilers with recovery boilers would not have been made at the rate they were if environmental regulations were not prodding the investment. They would have been made at a slower rate consistent with the economic life of the older boiler. Nevertheless, the industry was quick to capitalize on the investments to the best of its ability. Other industries provide similar examples of private industry's success in solving problems at the least cost to final users.

The goal of a physically and socially healthy environment is desirable, but the significant questions concern who will pay for the inputs needed to meet these goals and at what rate? How much can the economy absorb at any given time? This preoccupation has preempted the time of businessmen, economists, and politicians during the past ten years. While economists are wont to say that the means used to achieve these goals are a political rather than an economic concern, I believe this is too easy an "out" for them. If economists cannot help decide who is to pay and at what rate, who can?

Many economists are espousing the idea that the market price of items in the future reflect the "external" costs related to producing, using, and getting rid of products. These costs include cleaning up pollution in the productive processes, as well as solid waste management and other costs that society as a whole generally bears to support its consumption habits. The polluter and manufacturer should pay for discharging effluents into the streams and the air and adding to the nation's growing volume of solid waste. This payment is to be made through a tax based on the amount of effluent discharged or solid waste produced; it is labeled *internalizing the costs of pollution.* It sounds sensible, but in practice the proposal has many flaws. Our experience with energy teaches us that consumption habits are not easily changed. Very large increases in prices are needed to reduce the demand for many consumer goods. The areas of discretionary spending for the average consumer, after all, are simply not that large.

One flaw in the "polluter pays" argument is that the higher prices increase the tensions between producers and consumers and will result in demands for higher wage rates to compensate for these higher costs. It completely ignores the benefits accruing to the economic system based on the idea that the Consumer is King. When consumers make up their own minds on the relative merits of the quality and cost of goods, they pressure producers and cause quick adjustments in production. But when the customer is pressured through artificially induced higher prices which conflict with his values, he balks. After all, to raise the cost of toilet tissue, newspapers, and magazines is to hit at the basic budget of consumers, and that makes a program of government-induced price increases difficult to achieve. But instead of attacking the costly regulations, consumers helplessly harangue producers.

This policy fails on another count: the taxes drain cash from producers at a time when they are supposed to be investing heavily to reduce pollution; it means even more price inflation.

The nation is capable of producing environmental regulations that are compatible with a healthy environment at an affordable cost. Businessmen now recognize that they have a responsibility to help solve these problems if they wish to preserve the free choice economy they espouse. Under all circumstances consumers will have to pay more, but with better management of environmental pressures, the pace of advance can be much more gradual, the investment much more aggressive and balanced, and the planning base of the nation can remain sensitive to consumer needs as well as resource restraints.

It is astounding how quickly some economists have retreated to direct government intervention as the means for handling the changes in planning mandated by the new dimensions in the economy. These new factors include possible supply constraints, the quality of the environment, a faster pace of technological change, and greater worldwide interdependence. It may take time for the private sector to adjust to these new influences, but it eventually does adjust, and because the bottom line is always an important factor in business decisions, the results are generally the most efficient.

Thus capital formation is a necessary part of solving environmental and social problems. It permits the efficiency to help bear the cost of these needed changes in the system. So long as the need is synchronized with productivity, distortions and inflation are minimized.

CAPITAL FORMATION AND SHORTAGES

Two years ago the government established the Commission on Shortages and Supplies to examine the reasons for shortages in 1973-74 and to determine the vulnerability of the economy to such shocks in the future. Causes for shortages varied industry by industry, but in all cases the need for greater capital formation was stressed.

Energy has suffered from mismanagement at all ends. Environmental regulations, antinuclear power attitudes, price controls, and failure to use coal resources efficiently are among the many aspects of our energy problem. Despite the urgent and critical need for an energy program, the country still does not have one.

In this case the problem clearly centers on capital formation and the means to finance it. Some stress the need to decontrol prices to encourage more investment. Others maintain that use must be curtailed to match known supplies. Whatever is decided, massive amounts of money will have to be channeled into energy. However, the programs to date do not deal adequately with this need and, until they do, energy will remain a major factor of uncertainty contributing to sluggish investment in new facilities in other sectors of the economy. Reduced to its ultimate point, uncertainty over energy creates doubt over future growth rates of the U.S. economy and the need for more investments.

Further, the nation worries over waste and shortages and yet gives scant recognition to the birth of a new industry—resource recovery. Through investment in attractive and efficient facilities, local garbage can be mined for its most economic value—for recycling paper, metal cans, and bottles and for fuel after these reusable items are removed. Technology is lowering the cost of this process so that it is becoming an economically viable industry.

Capital formation is the key to preventing shortages while encouraging growth, as the Commission's studies so clearly conclude.

CAPITAL FORMATION AND INTERNATIONAL TRADE

Unlike European and Japanese economies, U.S. industry does not make major investments for export markets. At least, it seems that export markets do not figure heavily in most investment decisions. Our volume of exports is high in agriculture and heavy equipment where we have maintained good production gains through technology. We are low-cost producers in quite a few industries and are gaining in several more; increasing that edge over other countries is a fundamental challenge to the U.S. economy. Capital formation is the key.

Protectionist sentiment is rising again. The large increase in the number of antidumping cases is symptomatic of the problem. This is similar to the protectionist urge that led to the introduction of the Burke-Hartke bill in 1970. At that time U.S. industry had difficulty recovering from the 1969-70 recession, and labor unions blamed imports and the investment policies of multinational companies for their plight; they called for restrictions on both. It was relatively easy to combat the call for protectionism at that time by pointing out that (1) a return to normal growth rates in the U.S. and in the rest of the world would restore vigor to both international markets and to the U.S. economy and (2) a dollar devaluation was also needed. The devaluation and a resumption of faster growth actually occurred and the protectionist mood became subdued. This time the solution is not that simple; it will be more costly in time, money, and efficiency.

Energy figures heavily in the solution of the problem, but tariff and nontariff barriers are also receiving more attention. The U.S. must learn how to pay its imports bills through higher exports.

Often the impetus to a country's capital formation from imports is lost. Imports are considered a negative factor in investment. With the larger worldwide interdependence of supplies and the actions of multinational corporations in allocating resources efficiently, imports can actually increase investment. Foreign cars need servicing facilities and assembly operations. Electronic production is moving back to the U.S., although it will be under Japanese ownership and component parts may be made in other parts of the world. It would be interesting to see an updated study on the contribution of imports to capital spending.

CAPITAL FORMATION AND TAXING POLICIES

The lag in the recovery of plant and equipment spending has at long last focused attention on the fact that the current tax structure impedes capital formation. The reasons are many. I have alluded to some in other sections of this discussion. The U.S. Department of Commerce has shed much light on the overtaxation of profits resulting from mythical inventory profits and the undervaluation of replacement costs of facilities. *After these adjustments,* the effective corporate tax rate is about 51 percent and not the 40 percent calculated on the basis of reported profits.

The after-tax return on investment peaked at 10 percent in 1965 and is now down to 3.7 percent after adjustment for inventory profits and the undervaluation of replacement costs.

Although retained earnings plus depreciation have maintained a relatively stable share of gross sales, the cash flow generated is not sufficient to finance large increases in new investment. Without more confidence in the future, businessmen will be reluctant to increase debt. Equity markets are not an encouraging source of funds at present. Tax reductions are the obvious answer.

CONCLUSION

The vital signs of an economy are found in the capital formation sector. Lagging investment leads to inflation, inefficiencies, inability to meet basic requirements, and finally a crisis which then generates policies to reactivate capital formation. The experience of New York City and the British economy give ample evidence of this process.

The vital signs of the U.S. economy are still good but they could be better. The growth rate in spending for plant and equipment—excluding pollution control outlays and after adjustment for inflation—declined from 4.3 percent per year in 1965-70 to 3.3 percent in 1970-75 and is moving lower. The growth in the capital stock is falling behind the growth in the labor force, and productivity increases are smaller than in the past.

These are warning signs that cannot be ignored.

Investment reflects confidence and the willingness of savers to put their money into ventures that will yield an adequate return only over time. Present after-tax returns on investment in productive facilities are not competitive with other investment outlets. A reduction in taxes will improve their ability to compete.

The existence of a huge federal budgetary deficit to absorb savings acts as a competitor to capital formation. Liquidity does not necessarily create productive investments; instead it finds its way into government spending.

Energy is a prime mover in current investment decisions. It will force increases in investment of major magnitudes in all industries but it also creates uncertainty over the nation's future growth rates.

Communications technology has been changing rapidly during the past twenty years but the industry remains on the threshold of even further gains.

Tax cuts are needed and will help; initially, they may be used to speed up the replacement of existing facilities but these will eventually pressure new facilities investment. Capital goods industries are their own best customers, and it does not take too much to pressure expansion and investment in new capital goods industries.

Monetary policy must not be restricted by overreaction to money supply changes or fluctuations in interest rates. Economists must come up with some innovative ideas on how to maintain a steady velocity for spending.

Capital formation will help all jobs, skilled and unskilled.

Capital formation is the road to growth in a world of scarcity.

Capital formation is the only solid basis we now have for moderating inflation.

You must conclude from the above summary that I have a single dimension view of the solution to many of our problems. It may seem that I consider capital formation the panacea for the U.S. economy. I recognize that there are many facets to this question of growth; capital formation is only one. But what is clearly evident is that without more capital formation these problems will be solved only at the price of greater government intervention and slower economic growth. With more attention to capital formation, the solution can be achieved against a background of solid growth and real strength.

NOTES

1. *Federal Reserve Bulletin*, December 1977, p.A38.
2. *Survey of Current Business*, December 1976, p.29, and September 1977, p.2.

FOUR

Availability of Raw Materials

Bruce C. Netschert
Vice-President
National Economic Research Associates

"The World is so full of a number of things . . . "

At the outset, it should be noted that this analysis will be limited to *mineral* raw materials. Mineral fuels, which are raw materials in only a limited sense, are excluded since they are covered in Chapter 5. The availability of mineral raw materials will be considered on a global scale.

Although a few decades ago, especially prior to World War II, the mineral economics literature focused in the main on the problems of lack of self-sufficiency by individual nations and concern with whether or not they would have access to foreign sources of supply, such a preoccupation now seems quaint. The Japanese, with almost no mineral resources of consequence, have demonstrated how irrelevant such a circumstance is for a nation possessing the other means needed for economic growth. I assume, in other words, that there is generally free access to the world's mineral resources, at least in the non-Communist world; and I hope to demonstrate that to the extent an iron curtain may exist around the Communist world it is, in the last analysis, also irrelevant.

In the context of this lecture series, the title, "Availability of Raw Materials," implies a question: Will the availability of mineral raw materials impose any restraint on the continued economic growth of the

United States in the future? This chapter addresses itself to that question.

Those who hold pessimistic views on this question can be characterized as "Doomsdayers" while others who are more optimistic are known as "Cornucopians." As these labels suggest, the former say we are running out, the latter say we have nothing to fear for the indefinite future. The "Doomsday" position has a noble heritage in classical economic literature, well described by Barnett and Morse in their excellent book, *Scarcity and Growth*, as "the economic doctrine of natural resource scarcity":

> In economic terms, the belief seems to be that natural resources are scarce; that the scarcity increases with the passage of time; and that resource scarcity and its aggravation impair levels of living and economic growth. This set of simple and seemingly meaningful propositions epitomizes the dominant group views of layman and expert alike concerning the influence of natural resources upon economic welfare and economic growth.[1]

The purest expression of this doctrine in recent years is, of course, the Club of Rome's widely cited study, *Limits to Growth*.[2]

The Cornucopian view is that quantitative estimates of resources tend to be understated because of insufficient knowledge and conservatism; that technological advances in production with the passage of time "create" reserves out of previously unusable resources;[3] and that in the last analysis it is all a matter of *relative* scarcity and relative price. These several points are contained with varying emphasis in the Cornucopian literature,[4] and it is probably fair to say that Cornucopians would generally agree with this statement:

> . . . no physical shortages of raw materials exist in the world today and are not likely to exist in the foreseeable future. While a specific raw material is finite, there is no cause for concern about physical shortages because of the nature of raw materials and what they are used for.[5]

I declare myself at this point to be a confirmed Cornucopian, and in the remainder of this chapter I shall present a brief survey of those arguments supporting the viewpoint I find convincing.

AVAILABILITY OF MINERAL RESOURCES

The fundamental determinant of the availability of any mineral resource is, of course, its abundance in the earth's crust. Just as some people are more equal than others in certain societies, some elements are more abundant: iron, aluminum, and titanium, for example, are more abundant than gold, silver, and uranium. But relative abundance tells us nothing about availability. To be economically available, the element must occur in a deposit in which it is concentrated at something higher than the crustal abundance level (i.e., its percentage contribution to the total makeup of the earth's crust). Geologists and mining engineers define such occurrences as *ore*—mineral raw material that can be economically worked.

The ratio between crustal abundance and the minimum workable concentration (the "cutoff grade") is shown in Table 4.1 for a number of elements. The *Crustal Abundance* column shows the parts per million (ppm) of the earth's crust accounted for by each of the listed elements. Mercury, for example, accounts on average for 0.089 tons of each one million tons of the earth's crust. The *Cutoff Grade* column is also given in parts per million and, for mercury, shows that one million tons of ore would have to contain at least one thousand tons of mercury (i.e., a concentration of 0.1 percent) for it to be economincally workable. The *Ratio* column shows the ratio between the other two figures. Again, for mercury, it shows that the minimum concentration of mercury that is economically workable is 11,200 times the average concentration in the earth's crust.

It will be seen that, although there is a rough inverse correspondence between crustal abundance and the concentration ratio, there are many disparities. The low ratio for copper, for example, reflects the geologic characteristics of copper deposits and the technology that can be applied to them. The ratio for silver and gold, the two rarest elements on the table, is much lower than several far more abundant elements, reflecting the value of the precious metals.

It is also evident that there is extreme variation in the absolute level of the cutoff grade, or minimum workable concentration. Thus gold can be worked at an ore concentration of only a few ten thousandths of 1 percent, whereas iron ore must have a minimum content of 18.5 percent. This reflects the ratio of the value of the mineral commodity to

Table 4.1 Ratio of Cutoff Grade to Crustal Abundance of Selected Minerals

Element	Crustal Abundance (parts per million)	Cutoff Grade (parts per million)	Ratio
Mercury	0.089	1,000	11,200
Tungsten	1.1	4,500	4,000
Lead	12	40,000	3,300
Chromium	110	230,000	2,100
Tin	1.7	3,500	2,000
Silver	0.075	100	1,330
Gold	0.0035	3.5	1,000
Molybdenum	1.3	1,000	770
Zinc	94	35,000	370
Uranium	1.7	700	350
Carbon	320	100,000	310
Lithium	21	5,000	240
Manganese	1,300	250,000	190
Nickel	89	9,000	100
Cobalt	25	2,000	80
Phosphorus	1,200	88,000	70
Copper	63	3,500	56
Titanium	6,400	100,000	16
Iron	58,000	200,000	3.4
Aluminum	83,000	185,000	2.2

SOURCE: Earl Cook, "Limits to Exploitation of Nonrenewable Resources," *Science*, 20 February 1976, p. 678.

the cost of separating it from its ore. The high value of gold makes it economical to handle large quantities of waste material for each unit of quantity recovered, but it is also true that the recovery of gold from its ore is a simple matter; it occurs in the native state and is separated from the ore by a straightforward mechanical or chemical process. Aluminum, in contrast, is not only lower in value, but also its recovery involves a more complicated process and extremely high energy input.

The availability of a mineral resource is also determined by the nature and abundance of the deposits in which it occurs. Deposits of many metals—such as copper, lead, and zinc—commonly occur as

veins filling fractures, having been deposited from hot solutions cours-
ing through the fractures. Thus, deposits of these metals are one of the
products of the violent underground activity that accompanies mountain building: the intrusion of large bodies of molten rock and the frac-
turing and distortion of the existing rock by the forces responsible for
the intrusion. Other mineral deposits, such as common salt, gypsum,
and potash, were precipitated from ancient shallow seas as they
evaporated, forming large tabular layers or beds of great areal extent.
Still others, such as aluminum deposits, are "residuals," the result of
long, slow weathering of rocks under warm, moist climatic conditions
which broke down the original rock minerals and leached away the
siliceous material. Most of the world's large iron ore deposits are also
the residual product of weathering and occur in very old rocks in
which the original iron concentration is thought to have been the result of bacterial action.

This variability in the genesis of the ore deposits of the different
minerals means that some occur in many places around the globe, in
large deposits of wide areal extent; others occur in only a few places, in
small, localized deposits. Again, neither the given mineral raw material's frequency of occurrence of deposits nor the total content of those
deposits is necessarily correlated with relative crustal abundance.
Their location in a particular country, moreover, is fortuitous. In general, the smaller the area of a country, the smaller the number of
different mineral deposits it is likely to have and the greater the likeli-
hood of its having little or nothing in the way of mineral resource
endowment.

ROLE OF TECHNOLOGY

The second major determinant of mineral raw material availability
is technology, and its application to all the stages of resource exploitation, from discovery of the deposit to recovery and reuse after initial
use. From the viewpoint of mankind's activities, if a deposit cannot be
found it may as well not exist. The history of mineral exploration technology parallels that of all other technology—progression from the
simple and obvious to the use of increasingly more complex, subtle
(and expensive) techniques. Prior to the development of geological

science, exploration was little more than blind searching until one stubbed one's toe on the outcropping ore; many times this was the literal discovery event. As the understanding of geological processes and the genesis of ore deposits developed, it became possible to study the general geology of an area and to infer the likely existence of deposits of certain minerals. Exploration, nevertheless, was still limited to what could be seen at the surface. Such geological prospecting has been possible for only the past hundred years, roughly speaking.

In the 1920s, the oil industry pioneered the applicaton of geophysical exploration techniques, whereby it became possible to infer the underlying structure of the rocks from physical measurements taken at the surface. Beginning in the 1930s these techniques were applied to minerals other than petroleum, and during the period since World War II geophysical prospecting has become the universal and indispensable means of search. The physical phenomena that can now be applied to exploration include magnetism, gravity, electricity, seismics, radioactivity, and isotope ratios. The science of geochemistry is also employed, whereby surface waters and rocks are analyzed for their trace element content to provide clues as to what may lie beneath. The success of this technology is evident in the increasing proportion of discoveries of ore bodies with no direct surface indication whatever.

The most recent technologic addition to the exploration arsenal comes from space technology. Satellites are now providing images of the entire earth's surface taken at infrared wavelengths as well as those of the visible spectrum. The infrared images not only dispose of the problem of cloud interference but reveal geologic features not otherwise discernible. Significant discoveries have been reported through the use of this new information.[6]

All of this enhanced technological capability, moreover, has received a boost in effectiveness from advances in geologic science itself. In the past two decades the science has undergone a revolution as fundamental and far-reaching as the revolution in physics early in this century. Just as relativity theory brought together seemingly disparate and incongruous elements of knowledge in physics, so the theory of plate tectonics has unified areas of geological knowledge that previously defied a common explanation. Each of the continents is embedded in a plate of the earth's crust. These plates, plus others outside the continental areas, are in constant but imperceptible motion and apparently have been throughout much of geologic history. Collisions between plates and the events these produce constitute the long sought-for explanation of mountain building and other tectonic phemonena.

In the present context the importance of plate tectonics is that it provides evidence of a common origin for widely separated mineral districts and suggests that specific types of mineral deposits are associated with certain kinds of events in plate tectonics. The theory is still in its infancy, but already it has guided searchers in deciding where to look and where not to look. Plate tectonics contributed in this fashion to the discovery of copper deposits in New Guinea and has provided the basis for exploration in Turkey, Iran and Newfoundland.[7]

Reserves Versus Resources

Before discussing the application of technology to mining, let me first digress to a reconsideration of the matter of mineral concentration and ore deposits. We have seen that there is a wide disparity between crustal concentration and concentration in ore. *Ore*, you will recall, is defined as material that is economically workable. But what about the material with a concentration falling between that of ore and the crustal concentration? For many decades it was customary, among geologists and mining engineers, to use the terms *reserves* and *resources* in referring to quantitative estimates of mineral raw materials in the ground. It was understood by those in the mining industries that *reserves*, strictly speaking, referred only to known ore—that is, ore which had been proved to exist and which, by definition, could be profitably mined (with existing technology) at existing costs and prices. *Resources* was a broader, ill-defined term which included material known to exist that might be profitable at unspecified higher prices as well as "reserves" that had not yet been discovered, but were conjectured to exist.

This terminological ambiguity, which led to constant confusion in the published estimates of remaining mineral supplies in the ground, was finally resolved through the efforts of S. G. Lasky in the early 1950s.[8] Lasky proposed that the term *reserves* be used solely in its industry definition of known material, economically recoverable under existing circumstances, and that *resources* apply to the uneconomic or submarginal material. This distinction was adopted by professional geological societies shortly thereafter and was subsequently adopted also by the United States Geological Survey in what eventually came to be a more elaborate terminological scheme that need not concern us here.

The reserve-resource distinction still left some ambiguity, however. If resources referred to uneconomic material, how far did it go in covering the wide gap between crustal concentration and the concentration in ore? What was meant by an estimate that the remaining resources of a specific mineral amounted to X million tons? Did it include material at the crustal concentration and material as yet undiscovered? What economic circumstances were assumed?

In an effort to remove this ambiguity, in 1958 I proposed the term *resource base*, which I defined as the sum total of all of a specified mineral raw material contained within the earth's crust under a specified area, regardless of technologic feasibility of extraction and cost considerations, and including undiscovered as well as discovered occurrences.[9] I further proposed that resources be understood to include anything between reserves and the resource base, but that any estimate of resources include the technologic and economic assumptions on which it was based. The term *resource base* has been generally accepted, but I regret to say that resource estimates continue to be published with no indication of the assumed technologic and economic circumstances. Nevertheless, a considerable literature on mineral resource terminology has blossomed and the ambiguity that remains is comfortingly less than that which previously prevailed.[10]

Relationship Between Grade and Tonnage

I have engaged in this digression in order to show the larger implications of the application of technology to mining. Consider first the gap previously mentioned between crustal concentration and ore concentration. In a series of papers in 1950, Lasky pointed out that a plot of tonnage produced versus average grade for certain mines—notably those working a type of orebody known as porphyry copper deposits—revealed a mathematical relationship between grade (i.e., concentration) and tonnage. Tonnage increased exponentially with each unit decrease in grade.[11] Lasky hoped to show similar mathematical relationships for other minerals, but it became apparent that matters were not as "clean" as they were with the porphyry coppers. It is clear in any event that in some rough fashion the relationship holds for most minerals: the lower the concentration, the greater the total quantity of the mineral commodity in the resources down to that concentration level. This has important implicatons for long-term mineral supply: Higher prices and technological progress make possible the exploitation of mineral resources with a greater total content of mineral commodities than those previously worked.

Real Economic Costs

This is all well and good as an abstract statement, but what relevance does it have to the real world? Let us look at history. In 1959, Resources for the Future published a study in which O. C. Herfindahl investigated the long-term behavior of the real price of copper over the period 1870 to 1957. After an exhaustive and meticulous analysis, Herfindahl concluded:

> The deflated price of copper did not tend to rise or fall persistently in the period from about 1885 to World War I. Similarly, the record of the deflated price of copper since World War I discloses no persistent tendency to rise or fall.[12]

He took great pains to eliminate the effects of market control, so to the extent possible his price data reflected only cost. Thus, one can conclude that the real cost of copper did not rise over that period. There is nothing remarkable in that statement until one compares it with the grade of ore being produced, which declined from a level of 2.5 percent in the latter part of the nineteenth century[13] to 0.76 percent in 1957.[14] A decline of 70 percent in the grade of ore being worked had no effect on real price! Subsequently, Barnett and Morse found that for the extractive sector as a whole in the United States over the same period — 1870-1957 — " . . . the trend in the unit cost of extractive goods as a whole has been down — not up."[15]

Now, it is not at all clear that this happy state of affairs has persisted into more recent years; nor would I claim that it should be possible to repeat that performance into the indefinite future. I recognize that the real economic cost, including social costs, of mineral production, may have been rising in the past; since it is likely that in the future these external costs will increasingly be internalized, the statistical record of the future may differ from that of the past.

Nevertheless the record does suggest—and in my opinion, convincingly—that we should be able to work lower grade ores of all minerals in general in the future without an inordinate increase in real cost even if we are not fortunate enough to prevent an upturn. Over the long term, in other words, and allowing for the development of necessary technology, the supply curve for minerals is not highly inelastic and may even be elastic. The world is still our oyster when it comes to mineral raw materials.

Ordinary Igneous Rock As a Source

For those who still persist in worrying about our children's children's children's children in coming centuries there is Harrison Brown's comforting news about ordinary igneous rock, which occurs in inexhaustible quantities and contains concentrations of many mineral raw materials well above the average crustal abundance:

> One hundred tons of average igneous rock contain, in addition to other useful elements, 8 tons of aluminum, 5 tons of iron, 1,200 pounds of titanium, 180 pounds of manganese, 70 pounds of chromium, 40 pounds of nickel, 30 pounds of vanadium, 20 pounds of copper, 10 pounds of tungsten and 4 pounds of lead. Given adequate supplies of energy these elements could be extracted from the rock and it appears likely that the rock itself contains the requisite amount of energy in the form of uranium and thorium.

> One ton of average granite contains about 4 grams of uranium, and about 12 grams of thorium. The energy content of this amount of uranium and thorium, assuming nuclear breeding, is equivalent to the energy released on burning approximately 50 tons of coal. It seems likely that the actual processing of the rock can be accomplished at an energy expenditure considerably smaller than 50 tons of coal, with the result that it seems possible

to obtain a net profit from average rock and at the same time obtain a variety of metals which are essential to the operation of an industrial society.[16]

The Energy Trade-Off

There is, however, a joker in the cornucopia, which you may have noticed. Brown mentions the energy required to work the igneous rock. Grade and energy requirements unfortunately constitute a direct trade-off—the lower the grade, the more energy is needed to recover the mineral commodity in useful form. It takes 28 percent more energy to obtain aluminum from clay than from bauxite, its current ore. It takes 63 percent more energy to obtain titanium from titanium-rich soils than from rutile, its current ore. It takes 95 percent more energy to obtain copper from porphyry ore of 0.3 percent grade than from ore of 1.0 percent grade.[17]

To give you some idea of the magnitude of this effect, Census data show that in the decade 1963-72 the total energy consumption by the mineral industries[18] increased by 63 percent. Since the index of physical production for metal mining increased by only 30 percent and the index for nonmetals by 18 percent during the period, it is evident that the energy input per unit of output in the mineral industries is rising rapidly.[19]

Much of this increased energy use is expended *in handling waste material.* In 1973, the United States mineral industries [20] handled a total of 2.552 billion tons of material, of which 1.625 billion tons, or 64 percent, was waste. In comparison, in 1959—the first year for which the Bureau of Mines published comparable statistics—the industry handled 954 million tons, of which 452 million tons, or 47 percent, was waste. The scale of this materials-handling effort can be appreciated when it is realized that the mining industry, other than coal mining, currently handles four times as much material as does the coal mining industry alone and two and one-half times as much as the quantity the coal industry will be handling if it meets the goal of the Administration's National Energy Plan.

It is evident, then, that pursuing our mineral resources down the scale of concentration carries with it the penalties of exponentially increasing our energy consumption and massive disruption of the landscape. Long before resorting to mining ordinary igneous rocks, our mining efforts would be creating vast pits on the scale of some of the moon's modest-sized craters.

Given the raging controversy over the desirability of continuing our current rate of growth in energy consumption (which I have prudently excluded from this discussion), let alone increasing it, and given the emotional storms over current environmental impacts, these side effects, so to speak, of continuing to work ore of ever lower grade cannot be dismissed lightly. My intent here is only to emphasize that we have the resources to draw on if we wish to do so. Whether we *should* in view of the consequences is another matter, as is the output level which would prove economic were all external costs internalized.

THE MARINE ENVIRONMENT

But there is still another area of resources to which we can turn—those of the marine environment—which in one instance disposes of both the energy and environmental issues and in the second instance eliminates at least the latter. The first instance is the occurrence of nodules of certain elements on the sea bottom. (Some nodules are composed of phosphorite and constitute an immense resource for the manufacture of phosphate fertilizer.) I shall confine myself, however, to a discussion of the so-called manganese nodules, which have even larger implications. These manganese nodules which were formed by the precipitation of certain metals from the sea water and which have been found at locations throughout the world, appear to range in size from small grains to boulders and to average a few inches in diameter.[21] Heavy concentrations of nodules appear to cover the sea floor over thousands of square miles in the Pacific Ocean and in the southwestern North Atlantic.

The principal component of the nodules, manganese oxide (hence the name, manganese nodules), accounts typically for some one-third of the total composition. The composition is highly variable, but the content of other metals ranges as high as 2.5 percent copper, 2.0 percent nickel, and 0.2 percent cobalt in a given deposit.[22] Although knowledge of the total resources involved is still fragmentary, there is no doubt that the quantities of metals involved are staggeringly large. Moreover, the nodules are constantly growing through slow accretion, with the astonishing result that in some instances the total amount of metal being added to the nodules each year exceeds the world's annual consumption! Table 4.2 provides one estimate of the resource quantities and a comparison of the rate of accretion with United States consumption. The figures should be regarded as highly speculative, but even if they are highly optimistic, the implications for metal resource adequacy are profound.

Nor is this, like the mining of igneous rocks, a matter for the contemplation of the distant future. The concentraion of the metals in the nodules is so high that they constitute high-grade ore. Mining companies have been working on the necessary technology, and it is almost certain that but for the failure of the nations of the world to agree on a Law of the Sea to establish the legal basis for such deep-sea mining, there would be commercial nodule production today. For a while it appeared that the technology of processing might be a stumbling block, as the mineralogy of the nodules is complex and existing processing techniques could not handle it. But this, too, is reported to have been solved. Undoubtedly, the pioneering production ventures will have their difficulties, and it could be a decade or more after mining once starts before a truly viable industry is established. Nevertheless, it is hard to avoid the conclusion that the reserves of several metals will soon be multiplied many times.

The second instance of marine resources is the content of the oceans themselves. Seawater has a dissolved content of some sixty elements, all but a few in trace amounts. Given the total quantity of water, however, we are again dealing with large quantities of metals. Table 4.3 lists the ocean content of some of the metals. Only magnesium is present as more than a trace element, and this is, in fact, currently being produced commercially from seawater. Production of the others would involve the handling of truly enormous amounts of water, with associated large energy requirements for pumping, as well as some fancy extraction technology that does not exist. If anything, the seawater resources are even more remote, as a practical matter, than the igneous rocks. But they are there.

Table 4.2 Reserves of Metals in Manganese Nodules of the Pacific

Element	Amount of element in nodules (billions of tons)	Rate of U.S. consumption of element in 1973 (millions of tons/year)	Reserves in nodules at consumption rate of 1973 (thousand years)	Rate of accumulation in nodules (millions of tons/year)	ratio (Rate of accumulation/Rate of U.S. consumption)
	(1)	(2)	(1)÷(2) (3)	(4)	(4)÷(2) (5)
Magnesium	25	0.116	216	0.18	1.552
Aluminum	43	5.685	8	0.30	0.053
Titanium	9.9	0.0201[1]	495	0.069	3.450
Vanadium	0.8	0.006	133	0.0056	0.933
Manganese	358	2.140[2]	167	2.5	1.168
Iron	207	164.552	1	1.4	0.009
Cobalt	5.2	0.009	578	0.036	4.00
Nickel	14.7	0.198	74	0.102	0.515
Copper	7.9	2.437	3	0.055	0.023
Zinc	0.7	1.504[3]	0.5	0.0048	0.003
Molybdenum	0.77	0.041[4]	19	0.0054	0.132
Silver	0.001	0.007	0.1	0.0003	0.043
Lead	1.3	1.541	0.8	0.009	0.006

SOURCE: Columns (1) and (4): John L. Mero, "Will Ocean Mining Prove Commercial?" *Offshore*, April 1971, p. 127. Column (2): U.S. Department of the Interior, Bureau of Mines, *Minerals Yearbook*, 1974, vol. I.

NOTES: [1]Sponge Metal
    [2]Manganese Ore
    [3]Slab Zinc
    [4]Concentrate

Table 4.3   Ocean Resources—Selected Metals

Metal	Tons per cubic mile (1)	Total ocean content (tons) (2)
Magnesium	6,400,000	2.1×10^{15}
Strontium	38,000	12×10^{12}
Lithium	800	260×10^{9}
Zinc	47	16×10^{9}
Iron	47	16×10^{9}
Aluminum	47	16×10^{9}
Molybdenum	47	16×10^{9}
Tin	14	5×10^{9}
Copper	14	5×10^{9}
Uranium	14	5×10^{9}
Nickel	9	3×10^{9}
Vanadium	9	3×10^{9}
Titanium	5	1.5×10^{9}
Antimony	2	800×10^{6}
Silver	1	500×10^{6}
Tungsten	0.5	150×10^{6}
Chromium	0.2	78×10^{6}
Thorium	0.2	78×10^{6}
Lead	0.1	46×10^{6}
Gold	0.02	6×10^{6}

SOURCE: J. L. Mero, *The Mineral Resources of the Sea* (New York: Elsevier, 1964), Table II, pp. 26-27.

SCRAP AS A SOURCE OF SUPPLY

Straddling both supply and demand is the technology of secondary, or scrap supply. As shown in Figure 4.1, secondary supply is a large portion of total apparent consumption for lead, antimony, iron and steel, and is a modest portion for copper, zinc, tin, and titanium.[23] It is only a minor portion of the supply of magnesium, aluminum, and nickel.

These percentage figures for certain metals differ from those published elsewhere because I have not taken the data for total secondary

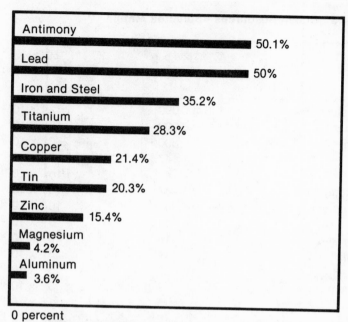

0 percent

Source: U.S. Department of the Interior, Bureau of Mines,
Minerals Yearbook, 1974, Vol. I.

Fig. 4.1 Secondary Supply as a Percent of Apparent U.S. Consumption of Selected Minerals in 1974.

supply but have distinguished between "new" and "old" scrap and used only the latter. New scrap is that metal generated during manufacture or use—the scrap produced during steelmaking, lathe turnings, the waste from metal stamping, and the like; it is promptly recycled and is thus part of a feedback loop, to use the current jargon. Old scrap, in contrast, is recovered from the nation's junkyards from durable goods that have come to the end of its useful life and from the scrapping of capital goods—buildings and structures, abandoned rail lines and cables, and so forth. For this scrap, the cycle through reclaiming is measured in years or decades, depending on the use.

Since new scrap return is so prompt (months, weeks, or even days), it constitutes no *net* addition to annual supply. All old scrap recovery, in contrast, is such a net addition. And, since the source of old scrap is the entire stock of durable goods in use, as the economy grows so does

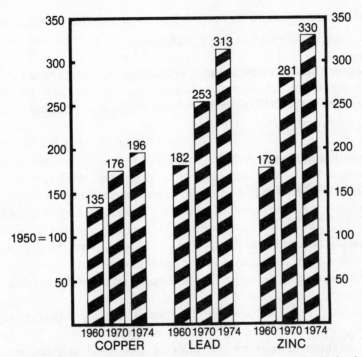

Source: Max J. Spendlove, *Recycling Trends in the United States: A Review*, Bureau of Mines Information Circular 8711 (Washington, DC.: U.S. Department of the Interior, 1976, p. 10.)

Fig. 4.2 Estimated Index: Stock in Use (1950=100)

the potential old scrap supply. The quantity of old scrap of any materials that is actually recovered in any year depends, of course, on the scrap price. These markets are notoriously volatile, and there can be wide fluctuations from one year to the next in the place of old scrap in total supply.[24] Figure 4.2 shows the estimated growth in the stock in use of copper, lead, and zinc for the period 1950-74.

The stock in use, however, is not the only determinant of potential secondary supply; the way in which a metal is used is equally important. Most uses of iron and steel, for example, are nondissipative: when the end product containing them is worn out, it can be thrown back in the melting pot, so to speak, and the metal reused. The uses of lead and zinc in pigments, on the other hand, are totally dissipative, as is the use of magnesium as protective anodes to prevent corrosion; there is no possibility of reclaiming the metal from such uses. Thus, it is the largely nondissipative use of iron and steel that is responsible for the high proportion of secondary supply in its total supply and the corresponding large dissipative uses of zinc that are responsible for the low percentage of reclamation of that metal.

Changing consumption patterns over the years have led to large changes in the secondary supply of different metals. At one time, lead had a wide use in roofing and cable sheathing from which it could be almost fully recovered. Substitution of other materials in these applications removed them as sources of secondary supply. In contrast, the replacement of lead oxide by titanium oxide as the pigment for white paint sharply reduced that dissipative use of lead. Now the high secondary recovery of lead is due to the predominance of battery use in the lead consumption pattern. Very few batteries are not traded in or removed from junked cars.

In the context of this discussion, the important point is that the secondary supply element is determined as much, if not more, by "outside" technology as it is by the price of the metal and the social desirability of reducing the drain on primary supply. In some instances, moreover, the economics are overwhelmed by institutional arrangements; such is the present situation with respect to aluminum. Wherever aluminum cans are now being recovered for remelting, it is a paying proposition; but for this to be feasible, garbage handling practices must be established that permit the segregation of the cans, and municipal operations do not always recognize economic opportunities. In addition, there must be some minimum level of consumption in a particular use that provides the economies of scale necessary to justify the scrap recovery.

The emergence of environmental preservation and energy conservation as social and political issues has brought with it a growing literature on the technology and economics of improved scrap recovery. The chief focus has been on the energy savings in aluminum (the energy requirements for secondary recovery are only 8 percent of the requirements for primary production),[25] and it is probable that only for this metal will we see a significant future growth of secondary supply as an element of total supply.

EFFICIENCY AND SUBSTITUTION

On the demand side, technology can increase the available supply of a mineral raw material, either directly or indirectly, in three ways. The first is through more efficient use. The supply of tin, for example, has been "stretched" through the development of means to use a thinner coating on tin cans. The amount of tin in a tin can produced in 1974 was only 42 percent of the amount in a 1950 can. Another example is the use of reinforced concrete (also known as "ferroconcrete"): by constructing buildings and structures of concrete instead of steel, the amount of steel required is reduced to the reinforcing rods in the concrete.

The second impact of technology on the demand side is through substitution. In the long run this is probably the most important factor of all in the response to the increasing relative scarcity of any particular mineral raw material, as it is the most likely response to increasing price. For the ferroalloys it is *the* answer to scarcity, since there is a large overlap in the properties the different alloy metals such as manganese, tungsten, chromium, cobalt, molybdenum, and vanadium give to steel. Although specific alloy metals may be preferred for certain uses of steel, none is truly irreplaceable, and the desired property or combination of properties can be obtained with other metals or combinations of metals.

History is replete with examples of substitution. Aluminum and titanium have replaced steel in light structural and specialized applications. Aluminum has replaced copper in some electrical uses, brass (a copper-zinc alloy) in hardware, and zinc in a host of small parts formed by the die-casting process. All of these metals have been replaced in turn by plastics. The use of silicon transistors replaced the many parts made of exotic metals in vacuum tubes. Copper is on the verge of being replaced by glass fibers in the telephone industry. We can confidently expect more substitution in the future, even if we cannot predict the specifics.

THE RULE OF SYNTHESIS

Finally, technology affects the available supply of mineral raw materials through synthesis. This applies, however, only to the nonmetals, since the development of metallic synthesis would require the commercial transmutation of one metal into another. The first example of synthesis of an important mineral raw material was in nitrates. At the beginning of the century, the world supply of this important basis for fertilizers and explosives came mostly from a single source—deposits of natural sodium nitrate in Chile. The combination of strategic vulnerability and growing fertilizer use led to the development of processes to "fix" nitrogen in usable form (as ammonia) from the nitrogen in the atmosphere. More recent examples are industrial diamonds and quartz crystal, used in metal working and radio frequency control, respectively. Commercial production of synthetic diamonds began in 1957 and is now twice natural production. The production of cultured quartz crystals, which began a year later, surpassed that of the natural product in 1971. Another example of lesser importance is the production of synthetic ruby and sapphire for watch and instrument bearings, which also occurred after World War II.

In citing these examples I do not mean to imply that we can expect future supply scarcities of any other nonmetallic mineral raw material to be met via the synthesis route. But technology, as I have noted, is unpredictable, and it is not unlikely that some other nonmetallics will be synthesized in the future. It is worth noting—subject as we are today to the din of the doomsday chorus—that all of the examples I have cited have two things in common: (1) the stimulus to commercial synthesis was a developing or prospective scarcity, and (2) the scarce natural material was replaced by a synthetic material made from ubiquitous and truly inexhaustible resource—the nitrogen of the atmosphere, carbon, sand, and aluminum oxide (which can be made from common clay). To be fair, however, I must admit that each synthesis is extremely energy intensive; yet, as my last word on the subject, only nitrogen is a large tonnage item.

INTERNATIONAL ACCESS TO SOURCES OF SUPPLY

Any discussion of mineral raw material availability would be incomplete without paying some attention to the subject of international access to the sources of supply and cartelization of the market. Access, the prime topic in the infant field of mineral economics during the

1930s and 1940s, will be discussed first. Looking back to the nineteenth century up through the early twentieth century, one could say that wars had been fought for and empires built on such access. Experience since World War II has shown, however, that the access problem disappeared with the empires. To be sure, the Iron Curtain remains around the mineral resources of the Communist countries, for whom autarky still retains its glitter and international trade is not a fact of economic life but a political tool. Nevertheless, with a few exceptions, notably the manganese of Russia and the tungsten of China, the world at large has gone about its business without relying in any large degree on the mineral resources of those countries.

As for the newly independent, as well as the older, countries of Latin America and Asia, most of which have in common a low level of economic development, nationalistic ambitions collide with economic realities. The world is more interdependent than it ever has been, and an undeveloped country embargoes the export of an important mineral resource in any form at its economic peril. This is not to say that there are no problems left. The undeveloped countries press for more processing of the raw material before it leaves their borders. A minor dictator satisfies his megalomania in one country, or a mystic seals his country's borders (as in Burma) for his own twisted reasons. But this cannot affect the world as a whole, as was true when nineteenth century empires shipped colonial production only to the mother country. In the broader sense, the matter of access is and will continue to be a collection of minor annoyances, not a major international issue.[26]

The Role of Cartels

As for the cartel problem, the situation at first glance looks ominous. The success of the OPEC cartel with oil dominates the scene, and the history of international mineral markets offers no encouragement. A partial list of the mineral raw materials in which there have been active international cartels in this century includes: aluminum, bismuth, copper, lead, manganese, molybdenum, nickel, potash, sulfur and tin. These cartels lasted for varying periods of time and achieved varying degrees of success in manipulating prices during their existence, but their number illustrates the clear propensity toward cartelization in international mineral activities.[27]

The propensity derives, of course, from the relatively limited number of large deposits of some mineral commodities, such as copper and tin, so that the collusion of only a few corporations or governments is necessary to establish cartel control. Given this fact, it is almost certain that there will be further attempts in the future, such as the recent abortive attempt by bauxite-producing countries to emulate OPEC. Since the maintenance of an artificially high price can be accomplished only through the restriction of production, the "availability" of the mineral raw material is thereby limited. Nevertheless, I do not think the possibility of cartel activity constitutes a serious threat to the availability of mineral supplies, for that very reason. The history of cartels demonstrates that they have ephemeral lives. Sooner or later, the differing interests of the participants (especially with respect to the allocation of production quotas) lead to internal conflict, and the more successful the cartel, the sooner other sources of supply spring into being under its price umbrella and eventually weaken it.

This appears to ignore the magnificent success of OPEC, but I view that cartel as an anomaly. The potentially disruptive issue of the allocation of production restrictions has been minimized by the dominance of Saudi Arabia in total OPEC productive capacity and its willingness to assume the major burden of whatever restrictions may be necessary. OPEC, moreover, could neither have achieved nor maintained its success without the full and eager cooperation of the international oil companies, which, through their own cartel arrangements, have insulated the OPEC countries from competition in the end markets. If the OPEC producers were fully integrated into those markets, they would be in a far more competitive situation, and their ability to preserve unity of action in the face of that competition would be correspondingly less. Still further, we must remember that the OPEC cartel is only four years old, and that the long-term economic forces generated by its actions have not yet had a chance to become apparent. I would not go so far out on a limb as to predict its imminent failure, but I would not be surprised if it were to happen sometime in the coming decade.

SUMMARY AND CONCLUSION

To sum up in one sentence: I find it difficult to conceive of a true scarcity situation developing in any nonfuel mineral during the coming decades, if ever. There are abundant low-grade resources of the major structural metals, iron and aluminum, for technology to work on. There are less abundant but still substantial low-grade resources of the nonferrous metals—copper, lead and zinc. But more important, there are abundant opportunities for substitution away from them as—and if—resource scarcity leads to sharp price rises. The ferroalloys have, on the resource side, the manganese nodules for some of them, and on the demand side, a high degree of intersubstitutability. For the nonmetallic minerals there are either abundant resources, as with potash, or the possibility of synthesis (I am not foolish enough to predict what will be synthesized next).

I conclude, therefore, that the availability of mineral raw materials will not impose constraints on the continued economic growth of the United States—and, for that matter, the world as a whole—for the indefinite future, if ever.

NOTES

1. H. J. Barnett and Chandler Morse, *Scarcity and Growth* (Baltimore: Johns Hopkins Press for Resources for the Future, 1963), p.49.

2. D. H. Meadows, *et al.*, *The Limits to Growth* (New York: Universe Book, 1972).

3. " . . . the increasing scarcity of particular resources fosters discovery or development of alternate resources, not only equal in economic quality but often superior to those replaced." Barnett and Morse, *Scarcity and Growth,* *p.10.*

4. See, for example, W. Beckerman, "Economists, Scientists, and Environmental Catastrophe," *Oxford Economic Papers* (New Series), November 1972, pp.327-44; H. E. Goeller and A. M. Weinberg, "The Age of Substitutability," *Science*, 10 February, 1976, pp.683-89; and D. B. Brooks, "Minerals: An Expanding or a Dwindling Resource?" *Mineral Bulletin MR 134* (Ottawa: Department of Energy, Mines, and Resources, 1973).

5. Commission on Critical Choices for Americans, *Vital Resources: Reports on Energy, Food and Raw Materials,* Critical Choices for Americans Series, vol. I (Lexington, Mass.: Lexington Books, 1977), p.131.

6. Space Applications Board of the National Research Council, *Practical Applications of Space Systems,* (Washington, D.C.: National Academy of Sciences, 1975), p.17.

7. A. L. Hammond, "The New Metallogeny: Impact on Exploration is Slow, but

Some See Good Prospects," *Science,* 12 September, 1975, pp.868-69. (Interestingly, a New Guinea copper mine was developed and equipped entirely by means of another new technology, helicopter transport from the coast to the remote mountain site.)

8. See, for example, S. G. Lasky, "The Concept of Ore Reserves," *Mining and Metallurgy,* October 1945, pp.471-74.

9. B. C. Netschert, *The Future Supply of Oil and Gas* (Baltimore: Johns Hopkins Press for Resources for the Future, 1958), p.4.

10. For an excellent summary of the development of mineral resource terminology, see: J. J. Schanz, Jr., *Resource Terminology: An Examination of Concepts and Terms and Recommendations for Improvement* (Palo Alto, Ca.: Electric Power Research Institute, 1975).

11. S.G. Lasky, "How Tonnage and Grade Relations Help Predict Ore Reserves," *Engineering and Mining Journal,* April 1950, pp.81-85. After further work, the U.S. Bureau of Mines concluded that for prophyry copper mines, tonnage doubles with each 0.1 percent reduction in copper concentration, "How Mining Will Have to Meet Expanding U.S. Mineral Needs," *Engineering and Mining Journal,* June 1966, p.138.

12. O. C. Herfindahl, *Copper Costs and Prices: 1870-1957* (Baltimore: Johns Hopkins Press for Resources for the Future, 1959), p.239.

13. B. S. Butler and W. S. Burbank, *The Copper Deposits of Michigan,* U.S. Geological Survey Professional Paper 144. (Washington, D.C.: U.S. Government Printing Office, 1929).

14. U.S. Bureau of Mines, *Mineral Yearbook, 1957,* vol. I (Washington, D.C.: U.S. Government Printing Office, 1958), p.426.

15. Barnett and Morse. *Scarcity and Growth,* p.199.

16. Harrison Brown, "Technological Denudation" (Background Paper No. 50, prepared for the Wenner-Gren Foundation International Symposium "Man's Role in Changing the Face of the Earth," Princeton, N.J., June 16-22, 1955), p.12.

17. Goeller and Weinberg, "Age of Substitutability," p.686.

18. Excluding coal, oil, gas, stone, and sand and gravel.

19. This energy consumption, moreover, does not include the use of explosives (which, interestingly, are never included in energy consumption statistics). In 1973, the U.S. mining industry (excluding coal) used 1.1 billion pounds of explosives. The data in this and the following paragraph are from the U.S. Bureau of Mine's *Minerals Yearbook* for the years 1960 and 1974.

20. See footnote 18.

21. Present knowledge is based on a few photographs and even fewer samples.

22. J. L. Mero, *The Mineral Resources of the Sea* (New York: Elsevier Publishing Company, 1965), p.179; and J. L. Mero, "Will Ocean Mining Prove Commercial?" *Offshore*, April 1971, p.128.

23. The lack of appropriate statistics made it necessary to compare secondary supply with total apparent consumption.

24. For a discussion of the economics of secondary supply, see Robert Adams, "Secondary Supply," in *Economics of the Mineral Industries*, ed. W. A. Vogely, *et al.*, Third Edition (New York: American Institute of Mining, Metallurgical and Petroleum Engineers, 1976), pp.208-23.

25. "Conservation of Energy," prepared by Harry Perry, of the Congressional Research Service, for the Committee on Interior and Insular Affairs of the United States Senate, Second Session of the 92nd Congress, Serial No. 92-18 (Washington, D.C.: U.S. Government Printing Office, 1972), p.71.

26. Access to the minerals of the ocean floor is, however, a potential problem that could become a major issue if the "Law of the Sea" regarding such access is not established.

27. Most of the earlier cartels are described in the pioneering study of mineral cartels: W. Y. Elliott, *et al.*, *International Control in the Non-ferrous Metals* (New York: MacMillan Co., 1937); and two of the volumes in the equally classic trilogy by G. W. Stocking and M. W. Watkins: *Cartels in Action* (New York: Twentieth Century Fund, 1946); and *Cartels or Competition?* (New York: Twentieth Century Fund, 1948).

FIVE

The Role of Energy

John C. Sawhill
President,
New York University

As other contributors to this book have made clear, future economic growth or stagnation will be determined by a wide range of policies and events. Not the least of these will be policies and developments in regard to energy. Yet, recognition of the emerging relationship of energy and the economy is a relatively recent phenomenon. In fact, if this lectures series had taken place ten years ago, it probably would not have included a paper on energy. Energy was, for most of the world, plentiful and cheap—a condition that contributed to tremendous postwar economic growth and that was almost universally regarded as immutable.

Although warning signs began to appear at the beginning of this decade, energy continued to be an all but negligible budget item for both the business community and the private citizen, and United States energy policy was largely concerned with restricting oil imports. With the oil embargo of 1973-74 came the first popular recognition that something had gone awry, although there was much dispute as to the "reality" of the energy crisis, its causes, and its solution.

Obviously, as debate in Congress over the past four years has amply demonstrated, there continues to be much confusion over appropriate responses to the crisis, despite growing recognition that it is, in fact, real and that it poses immense economic threats for the future. Some people regard it as a problem of security from arbitrary curtailment of oil imports; others tend to focus upon the financial difficulties that such imports impose. Increasingly, however, the crisis is being perceived as a series of problems arising from a growing supply-demand imbalance, and its solution defined as managing the transition to new energy sources. Indeed, many people are becoming convinced that the energy problems of the last four years and of the years immediately ahead do not constitute the "crisis" and that the true energy crisis is further down the road, when supplies of oil and natural gas begin to fall short of demand. It is this somewhat more distant crisis—one that involves not just a question of economic growth versus economic stagnation, but of economic growth versus economic collapse—that I will address in this paper.

Despite much of the surprisingly parochial tone of the debates that have been taking place in the United States over the past few years, the nature of this problem is international in scope, and discussion of the effect of a U.S. energy crisis on the U.S. economy misses the point. The U.S. economy is enmeshed in the world economy, as the record U.S. balance of trade deficit in 1977 and the accompanying record decline in the value of the dollar so clearly illustrated. And, increasingly, the prominent feature of that relationship is imported oil. The 1977 deficit of about $27 billion would, in fact, have been a surplus of perhaps $15 billion, but for the costs of imported oil. This, of course, reflects only the U.S. perspective; in other nations more dependent upon imported oil the economic risks of that dependence are even greater. The problem, then, is inextricably global, and meaningful consideration of it must take place in an international context that includes its implications for rich and poor oil producers and rich and poor oil consumers.

As a prelude to consideration of the problem, it is valuable to note that responses by the major oil importers to the 1973-74 embargo and dramatically higher oil prices have been relatively ineffective thus far. The United States, as the world's largest oil importer, reversed its trend of rising import levels only briefly—more as a result of recession than positive policy—before resuming the pattern that had developed prior to the embargo. In 1977, of course, the United States imported more oil at greater expense than ever before. In Europe both energy consumption and oil imports have been rising since 1975, suggesting that there, too, the drop that occurred in the wake of the embargo was induced by recession rather than any fundamental changes in end-use.

Although the impact on Japan caused the first decline in gross national product since the end of World War II and an accompanying reduction of oil imports through 1975, economic recovery and increasing oil imports resumed the following year. More significantly, little has been accomplished by the governments of these countries, especially in the United States, in the formulation of policies to deal with these trends.

Nor have the responses of international institutions been significantly more encouraging. The emergency allocation program of the International Energy Agency (IEA) now provides some useful insurance against short-term supply interruptions. However, the problems of a drawn-out confrontation with large supply cutbacks or of a chronic supply shortfall remain unaddressed. And although the Organization for Economic Cooperation and Development (OECD), the World Bank, the International Monetary Fund (IMF), and the private banking sector appear to have coped thus far with the problem of managing the burden of distributing and financing the higher oil deficit, doubts persist as to the capacity of the international financial system to accommodate future strains, unless changes are made.

The inadequacy of these responses to date, more than four years after the embargo, becomes all the more ominous when one considers the outlook for world oil supplies over the next ten to twenty years. I will first discuss that outlook on the basis of several recent studies, then briefly consider some of the economic implications of these forecasts, and, finally, suggest some strategies that might help the United States and other countries avert the potentially devastating effects of a sudden worldwide shortfall of petroleum in the years ahead.

CURRENT OUTLOOK FOR WORLD OIL SUPPLIES

Recently several major studies have been published which re-emphasize the seriousness of the energy situation by presenting a series of world oil supply-and-demand forecasts based on alternative assumptions about economic growth, producer-nation pricing and production decisions, and consumer-government actions in conservation and restructuring national energy production and distribution systems.[1] Although these studies differ in many respects, they coincide sufficiently in their central conclusions to draw from them a clear, and rather dramatic, picture of the challenges facing the United States and other oil-importing industrialized nations.

The OECD Study

The most widely known of these studies, prepared in 1976 by the Secretariat of the OECD, develops four scenarios:

1. A "Reference Case" scenario, which assumes a continuation of current consumption and production trends and the successful implementation of existing energy policies. The reference case assumes Gross National Product (GNP) growth in OECD countries of 4.3 percent (to 1980) and 4.1 percent (to 1985) and forecasts net OECD oil imports at about 35 million barrels a day by 1985. This scenario, according to the authors, "implies strenuous effort, in the form of considerable capital mobilization and reduced energy consumption. The lesson of the past three years is that this is an achievement that cannot be taken for granted."
2. A "Slow Growth Case," which assumes GNP increases of 3.8 percent (to 1980) and 3.6 percent (to 1985) plus successful implementation of existing policies. This scenario would lead to OECD import needs of 31.9 million barrels per day by 1985.
3. A "Fast Growth Case," which also assumes successful implementation of existing policies, but which is based on GNP growth of 4.8 percent (to 1980) and 4.6 percent (to 1985). In this case, OECD import needs would jump to 38.8 million barrels per day by 1985.
4. An "Accelerated Policy Case," which assumes the same growth rates as the Reference Case, but assumes that maximum conservation is achieved, indigenous oil is developed rapidly, and all alternative fuels expand significantly. OECD import needs in this scenario fall to 24.4 million barrels per day by 1985.

All of these OECD scenarios assume that prices will remain constant in real terms at 1976 levels and use economic growth estimates which were revised downward from the first OECD energy forecast completed in 1975. Estimated growth in energy consumption was also revised downward, and future growth is assumed to be less rapid than in the past.

With respect to oil supply, the OECD study suggests that by 1985 members of the Organization of Petroleum Exporting Countries (OPEC) may have expanded their rated production capacity to as much as 45 million barrels per day from present production capacity of about 39.2 million barrels per day, "but then as now the margin between the rated capacity and the exporter's desired level of output may be quite large. This margin could produce a close and uncertain balance between crude liftings and the demand for exports."[2]

Central Intelligence Agency Study

Another study, published by the U.S. Central Intelligence Agency (CIA), is decidedly more pessimistic. It estimates required 1985 OPEC production of between 47 and 51 million barrels per day, levels that may well prove exaggerated. A principal discrepancy between it and the OECD forecasts is the CIA's estimate that the Soviet Union and Eastern Europe as a region will change from a net exporter of nearly 1 million barrels per day now, to a net importer of 3.5 to 4.5 million barrels per day by 1985.

Both analyses, however, point to the large and growing role that the U.S. may play as a major consumer (and importer) of petroleum supplies. With U.S. imports accounting for an increasingly larger proportion of required OPEC production, it is clear that the seriousness of the U.S. commitment to expand domestic supplies, convert existing oil-fired boilers to coal, and curtail demand growth must be carefully evaluated in determining the requirements for a global energy strategy.

Both reports also draw attention to the critical question: to what extent would Saudi Arabia be able or willing to continue to expand production above the 8.5 million barrels per day it has previously set as an upper limit in an effort to ease the upward pressure on prices? CIA analysts feel that an enormous gap may materialize between projected demand and non-Saudi OPEC production. To meet the demand for OPEC production projected for 1985, Saudi production would have to rise to 17 to 24 million barrels per day. Even the lowest of these figures is double current production. The CIA estimates that maximum Saudi capacity by 1985 may reach, at most, 18 million barrels per day—current capacity is just over 11 million barrels per day—which, if produced, would push Saudi annual revenues (at current prices) to nearly $100 billion—or about ten times the value of all Saudi Arabia's current imports.

Within the Saudi government there is strong opposition to raising production further because of the lack of need for additional revenues and the feeling that high production rates only exacerbate the strong inflationary pressures currently prevailing within the country. At the same time, there is a recognition on the part of many Saudi leaders that they are ultimately dependent on the West for an economic climate in which their surplus funds can be invested safely and a political climate in which progress toward a Middle East settlement can be achieved.

For this reason, the Saudis have generally acted as a moderating force in OPEC price negotiations. The Saudi attempt in early 1977 to hold the 1977 crude oil price increase to 5 percent and the Saudi leadership in establishing an apparent 1978 oil price freeze are only the latest in a series of similar moves since 1973. Yet it is difficult to envision a policy of continued unrestrained increases in production without definite indications on the part of oil-importing nations that this claim on Saudi resources will be limited in time and will be securely compensated. In the short run, obviously, progress in resolving the Arab-Israeli conflict and in stabilizing the value of the dollar will affect the Saudi commitment to current and future high levels of production.

Workshop on Alternative Energy Strategies Study

The recently published report of the Workshop on Alternative Energy Strategies (WAES) tends to support the more pessimistic conclusions of the CIA study. This report, which is more comprehensive than the other two and focuses more on the 1985-2000 period, concludes that the supply of oil may fail to meet increasing demand well before the year 2000—most probably between 1985 and 1995—even if energy prices rise 50 percent above current levels in real terms.[3] Additional constraints on oil production, such as environmental restrictions in the U.S. and the reluctance of the Saudis and certain other exporting nations to expand capacity, could hasten this shortage and thereby reduce the time available for action on alternatives. Slower than anticipated energy demand growth could delay, but not prevent, the shortage.

The WAES report, like that of the OECD and the CIA, underscores the important position of Saudi Arabia and the U.S. in the world supply-demand picture, and cites "the critical interdependence of nations in the energy field" as requiring "an unprecedented degree of international collaboration in the future" as well as "the will to mobilize finance, labor, research and ingenuity with a common purpose never before attained in time of peace." The authors point out that "failure to recognize the importance and validity of these findings and to take appropriate and timely action" could create major political and social difficulties that could cause energy to become a focus for "confrontation and conflict."[4]

NEW SUPPLIES REQUIRE LONG LEAD TIME

A consideration that is emphasized heavily in these and other energy forecast studies is the *very long lead time that is required to expand energy supplies*. The record of the past half-century suggests, for example, that it is becoming increasingly difficult and expensive to find and produce oil and natural gas. More than thirty-five years elapsed between the discoveries of the East Texas field and the next major find in the United States, Prudhoe Bay on the North Slope of Alaska. And the lead times in bringing new fields into actual production are lengthening. Prudhoe Bay was discovered in 1968, and output did not start until 1977. In a more accessible area, such as the Gulf of Mexico, at least five years will elapse between the discovery of the most recent major find—Shell's Cognac Field—and the start of production in 1980.

These lead times are not confined to North America. The North Sea and the Middle East have experienced similar five-to-ten-year lead times and the frontier areas even longer. Nor are long lead times confined to oil and gas. Coal mines take four to eight years to bring into production; nuclear power six to ten years in Europe and Japan, and ten to twelve years in the United States. Thus, an electric utility that wants to have a major new nuclear plant on line and smoothly operating in 1990 must make the decision to proceed with the project in 1978.

Long lead times also are necessary to implement major energy conservation efforts, such as replacing energy inefficient capital equipment in industry and agriculture, improving the gasoline mileage of a nation's automobile fleet, and reinsulating existing commercial and residential buildings.

The implications of these lead times are clear. The world cannot wait until a "scramble for oil" occurs before taking the necessary actions to avoid sharp price increases and the economic and political difficulties which would inevitably accompany such increases. By then, it would have to close the supply-demand gap, and the world would have no alternative but to accept the consequences of higher oil prices.

STUDIES PROVIDE PROBABLE PATTERN OF FUTURE

In considering a range of future possibilities, it is always important to anticipate "surprises" that might significantly alter the projected outcome. Are there any events or discoveries that would invalidate or force a change in the image of the future suggested by the studies under consideration? Four of these seem pertinent here:

1. An extended worldwide recession;
2. A series of major new discoveries of regular oil fields in the 10-billion-barrel-or-more (recoverable) range;
3. A technological breakthrough that would make it possible within a short time to significantly expand supplies from known hydrocarbon deposits, for example, in the area of secondary recovery or in shale oil or tar sands extraction;
4. Rapid and unanticipated success of ongoing conservation programs throughout the world and particularly in the U.S., or the possibility that current demand forecasts seriously overstate future demand growth.

The first of these is obviously undesirable, although it might be precipitated by a new embargo, an oil squeeze associated with another Arab-Israeli war, or another sharp and sudden oil price increase. The second seems unlikely. Only nineteen such fields have been discovered in the last 100 years. Currently, about 60 percent of the world's oil reserves outside of the Communist countries is concentrated in the Middle East, and most of the remaining regions that might yield such resources have been evaluated by sophisticated seismic techniques or exploratory wells, with no evidence of another "Middle East" being found. The total amount of hydrocarbon reserves in the world, it is true, remains very uncertain, and the opinions of qualified experts vary widely on the subject. What is important, however, is that reserves of recoverable petroleum—in quantities sufficient to invalidate the projections discussed here—are indicated neither by available geological knowledge nor by past patterns of additions to reserves.[5] Technological breakthroughs seem more likely, but not in time to alter significantly world output levels by the mid- or even late 1980s.

With respect to the last of these "surprises," unprecedented achievement in conservation, there appears to be little basis for optimism. Certainly, the record since 1973 does not provide much encouragement in this regard. In the United States, in particular, the upturn in the economy has brought a startling renewal in the growth of energy consumption, despite the post-1973 crisis and growing dependence on imports. The current demand growth forecasts may well prove to be too high, and the quantity of energy desired may prove to be more responsive to higher prices over the next several years than was experienced in the 1973-77 period. But it would be surprising indeed if current demand forecasts were so wide of the mark as to negate the basic thrust of this analysis.

Core Assumptions for Energy Policy

On the basis of these and other studies of world energy prospects, it is possible to draw together a cluster of core assumptions which represents a prudent foundation for energy policy decisions, both national and international, in the United States and other oil-importing industrialized nations. These include the following:

1. Assuming a continuation of current energy consumption and production trends, there is a possibility of a serious shortfall of international petroleum supply, perhaps as early as the mid-1980s, leading to sharp oil price increases. The approach of such a shortfall may be obscured by production increases in the North Sea and Alaska.

2. Two countries, the United States and Saudi Arabia, by their actions can have a major independent influence on the world energy picture. In each case, action to avoid sharp price changes will require significant adjustments in current practices and policies: Saudi Arabia must choose to increase its export capacity beyond levels currently planned and beyond levels which might be more consistent with maximizing the economic return on its depleting resources; the United States must curtail significantly

its growing dependence on imported oil. Because of the long lead times involved in expanding energy supply and restructuring demand, failure of both to act may assure a new crisis within a decade; decisive action by either may purchase critically important time for adjustment.

3. Avoidance of a supply-demand imbalance will require vigorous policies designed to expand energy supply and to reduce consumption and waste in all the oil-importing countries. It will also require more permanent and widespread cooperation between suppliers and the major importing countries than has heretofore been the case.

4. We are involved in a global transition in the energy base of industrial civilization which may require costly and controversial alterations in lifestyles, modes of production, basic social values, and political organization. Measures taken to prevent a shortfall crisis—which could occur less than a decade hence—represent only the first of many difficult steps that must be taken in coming decades if economic welfare is to be secured. Such steps should, therefore, be initiated even if a shortage does not materialize due to forecasting error or the occurrence of one of the surprises listed earlier.

IMPLICATIONS OF THE WORLD OIL OUTLOOK

In order to underscore the seriousness of the supply-demand imbalance suggested by recent studies of the world oil outlook, it is instructive to consider briefly some of the economic problems it might cause. On the basis of what we now know, it seems likely that world oil supplies will remain in rough balance at current prices at least until the early 1980s, unless Saudi Arabia decides to cut production sharply. The most probable scenario is that North Slope oil will add 1.2 million barrels per day to U.S. production in 1978-79, and the North Sea will add 3 to 3.5 million barrels per day to Western European production by 1980. These additions should be adequate to meet rising demand and offset declining production from older fields, with the net result that the call on OPEC oil for the next five years will remain relatively stable.

Sometime in the 1980s, however, virtually all of the OPEC producers except Saudi Arabia will likely be producing at, or near, their officially imposed limits, and the world will have to look to the Saudis to provide the incremental supplies. The OPEC members which absorb internally most of their revenues, (the so-called "high absorbers,") now produce—and will continue to produce—at maximum capacity and, therefore, will be more likely to press even harder for price increases in the future, since higher prices will be the only avenue they have for increased revenues.

Impact on Developed Economies

The economic and political consequences of a rapid price rise could prove difficult indeed. For the developed economies it would mean a reduction in growth, an acceleration of the rate of inflation, a large international payments disequilibrium, and a dramatic increase in actual resource transfers to the oil exporters. Although the full effects of the first (1973) price crisis remain to be assessed, current estimates are that short-term reduction in GNP was on the order of 2.5 percent in the U.S., 2.7 percent in Europe, and 4.2 percent in Japan while inflation was accelerated by some 3 percent.[6] And, of course, oil importing countries have paid more than $350 billion in oil import bills since 1973.

Although the advanced industrial economies demonstrated considerable resilience in handling money and resource transfers caused by the quintupling of petroleum prices, many experts feel the world economy has been rendered more fragile and is less capable of absorbing another shock of such magnitude. Indeed, some argue that the current inability of many OECD countries to meet forecasts for economic growth made in the early 1977 can be traced to economic dislocations caused by higher energy prices.

Impact on Less Developed Countries

For the Less Developed Countries (LDCs) which must import oil, the impact of sharp price increases could be even greater—amounting in some cases to a virtual collapse of development programs. As one study has concluded, the cost of the recent price increases to oil-poor LDCs was $10 million in 1974, or about 1.7 percent of their combined

GNP. To this direct impact must be added the effect (to the extent that it was oil-induced) of the recession on demand for LDC exports in developed countries and of the increases in the cost of manufactured imports as these were passed through by the developed country exporters.[7]

The combined effect of these changes on the average economic growth rates of nonoil exporting LDC economies was pronounced. By 1975, the favorable 6 percent growth rates experienced in the early 1970s had been almost halved. To accomplish even that reduced growth performance, heavy reliance on external financing in the private capital markets of the advanced countries and increased official aid flows were needed. The net transfer of financial resources to nonoil exporting LDCs almost doubled between 1971-73 and 1974-76, and almost 40 percent of the net flow of financial resources to LDCs in the latter period represented increased credits from Western (mainly U.S.-based) commercial banks. In addition, major international loans were arranged for Italy and the United Kingdom (from approximately $20 billion in 1971-73 to over $37 billion in 1974-76).

The concern over the indebtedness of LDCs to commercial banks and the capacity of borrowers to receive and ultimately repay that debt was an inevitable result of these changes in international financial flows. Although it is true that the current account deficits of the nonoil producing LDCs are expected to decline from the $28.7 billion peak of 1975 to about $17 billion in 1977 and 1978, these deficits will continue at historically high levels for many years. And, equally disturbing, the deficits of the LDCs with the lowest per capita incomes are expected to increase.

Private financial institutions now hold over $35 billion of LDC long-term debt—up from $13 billion in 1973. And banks hold $76 billion of total LDC debt—up from $33 billion in 1973. Given this rate of increase in LDC borrowing from the private sector, it is difficult to see how the private banking system can continue to handle even currently anticipated LDC debt without support from governments and international agencies, such as the International Monetary Fund (IMF). A further doubling or tripling of oil prices obviously could not be accommodated by a system of debt relationships already under such serious strain. As a consequence, the poorest LDCs might be forced to curtail key sectors of economic activity, especially the more energy-intensive sectors. And, since the current average ratio of energy consumption to GNP growth is unusually high in countries undergoing rapid growth or "takeoff" (1.8 to 1, compared to the World Bank's estimate of .99 to 1 for developed countries), even countries with the more successful development strategies might suffer. Consequently, there is a major need to strengthen the capacity of various international institutions to accommodate this strain, and some specific suggestions will be made subsequently.

Political Strains

The political strains and instability to be expected from an economic crisis of the kind considered here are more difficult to delineate. Not all of the governments of the industrialized world are stable and strong enough to withstand such an economic shock without serious political ramifications. A sudden scarcity of energy, resulting in large price increases, could—under the most pessimistic energy-supply scenarios—curtail growth rates, increase unemployment, intensify ideological cleavages, and accentuate conflict over the distribution of wealth. The governments of LDCs, less institutionalized and therefore more sensitive to economic failure, would probably suffer even greater disruption under these circumstances.

Without effective advance cooperation among the industrialized countries, sharp energy price increases could also place heavy strain upon the alliances and informal ties that bind them together. Wide disparities in resource endowment and economic strength already predispose some governments to fashion distinctive "national" solutions to problems of energy dependence and money and resource transfers. An energy alliance system designed to control the short-term effects of an embargo can hardly be expected to contain the centrifugal forces generated by the kind of crisis considered here.

Furthermore, should the CIA forecast regarding the entry of the Soviet bloc into the international oil market as a major importer prove accurate, the projected shortfall crisis might also have a serious impact upon a range of issues in Soviet-American relations. Fortunately, the timing implicit in the CIA forecast may well prove mistaken; it would mean a swing of approximately $40 to $50 billion in Soviet balance of payments (at current prices), and a change of this magnitude is likely to be more than the Soviet government would find tolerable. However, it is clear that at some point the Soviets will begin to compete for oil imports.

Finally, it is important to recognize that the effects of economic dislocation—and resulting social and political unrest—on OPEC countries would also be serious. The suppliers depend on their ties with the industrialized world for the achievement of many of their economic, political, and strategic objectives. The kind of crisis described here threatens their oil revenues and their foreign investments; it might undermine the political and military support they receive from the West as well. Thus, suppliers may face a situation in which they are forced to choose between higher current income and greater risk of political and economic instability which could threaten their longer-range interests.

These speculations about the possible consequences of an unmanaged petroleum-supply shortfall—if they turn out to be correct—are sobering indeed. Such consequences are not necessarily inevitable. But it has become clear that successful management of the transition to a world of high-cost energy, including coping with supply problems of the kind anticipated in this analysis, could require both significant domestic policy adjustments and an unparalleled degree of international cooperation. And, because of the long lead times involved, we cannot afford to wait until the crisis has arrived to take the actions necessary to deal with it, but we must anticipate the problem and take these actions well in advance of the actual occurrence of physical shortages.

STRATEGIES FOR THE FUTURE

The problems that the United States and other major oil-importing nations face in managing the energy transition of the next decade may be viewed in three categories. First, the short-term, immediate problem is to assure the security of an adequate petroleum supply to enable us to cope with potential supply disruptions arising from an embargo, war in the Middle East, terrorism, a natural disaster, et cetera. Secondly, the problem for the intermediate-term is to assure that the international monetary system can continue to accommodate debt and payment demands. Thirdly, the long-term problem is, through a variety of strategies, to make the transition in the late 1980s or early 1990s to new energy sources and to do so without experiencing the potentially devastating sudden price increases discussed earlier.

Short-Term Strategies

The immediate need for assuring adequate petroleum supply must be met by strengthening the oil-stockpiling programs of the importing countries and by continuing to develop the special relationship that has emerged between the United States and Saudi Arabia.

In regard to the former, although members of the International Energy Agency (IEA) have agreed to attain a ninety-day supply in stock by 1980, the stockpiles of certain European countries and Japan should be increased.[8] In addition, opportunities to make stockpiling easier or cheaper should be explored; for example, the United States might provide storage facilities for Japan as part of an Alaskan "oil-swap" arrangement.

In regard to Saudi Arabia, we must continue to foster orderly resolution of the Arab-Israeli conflict and, thereby, political stability in the Middle East. In addition, we should address the concerns over worldwide inflation of Saudi Arabia and other producers whose export revenues greatly exceed their current cash needs. It is widely believed in such countries that the value of oil in the ground is not eroded by inflation, and that its real value will increase more rapidly than other secure investments. The creation of guaranteed indexed bonds issued by the U.S., the IMF, or some other appropriate international agency could make the early sale of oil more attractive than a later sale because investment of the proceeds could be protected against inflation. Obviously, development of such an approach would take time. However, with inflation generating genuine and possibly increasing concern, a near-term test of such a device might be appropriate.

Intermediate-Term Strategies

The international monetary system has thus far accommodated the strains placed upon it by increased oil imports and prices. Although some steps have been taken to handle the current level of demand, the system should be further strengthened to assure adequate management of the increasing volume and nominal value of international transactions. For example, the IMF should be strengthened as the focal point of short-term financing by a 25 percent increase in its quotas, and certain other changes should be made to strengthen the capability of it and private institutions to provide intermediate-term financing. In addition, the IMF "Supplemental Financing Facility" should be rapidly ratified and implemented with a significantly increased capacity and an expanded membership to include additional OPEC members and some oil-importing semiindustrial LDCs.

Also, the growing financial problems of the LDCs, alluded to earlier, should be addressed. Funds available for long-term development from the advanced industrialized countries have, in many instances, not kept pace with the rate of inflation. Such countries should commit themselves to raising their economic assistance to UN targets of .7 percent of GNP over the next five years. Countries with balance-of-payments surpluses, strong currencies, and full employment should move more rapidly toward that target.

In addition, the mix of assistance flowing through international organizations should be increased. Funds for the International Development Association should be replenished to provide at least $10 billion of soft-loan capacity over the next seven years. Also, a major increase in capital for the International Finance Corporation should be approved. Finally, the capital base of the World Bank should be increased to remove constraints on lending to higher income LDCs. These actions would tend to depoliticize long-term development financing and limit the required increase in lending from bilateral aid agencies.

Consideration should also be given to establishment of a multilateral "cofinancing" guarantee facility through which the OECD and OPEC countries might guarantee against default a limited volume of new bond issues or loans to countries which meet certain criteria. Such an arrangement could ease the transition from official development assistance to private financial markets for certain countries.

Long-Term Strategies

The foregoing steps should enable us to deal with some of the problems that will arise between now and the time when the oil "crunch" could take place. Consideration will now be given to a series of strategies that could help avert the "crunch" and provide a gradual and orderly transition to the era of higher-priced energy that lies ahead.

PRICING STRATEGIES

Part of the problem that the major oil-importing nations have faced in developing energy policy during the past several years is the lack of agreement on energy pricing. As a result, prices of liquid hydrocarbons and other energy sources lack uniformity and, in a number of instances, remain below world market levels.

Raise Prices to World Market Levels

Some governments—notably the United States and Canada—have been reluctant to permit domestic prices for oil and natural gas to rise to world market levels because of anticipated adverse consequences on their domestic economies and concern about the impact of rapidly rising prices on certain income groups. Other governments maintain electricity rates at artificially low levels. Yet, such policies have been one of the principal factors contributing to public uncertainty about the very nature of the energy crisis. U.S. consumers, for example, seeing that *real* domestic gasoline prices even today remain below 1950 levels, and receiving no clearcut signals about future prices, have been reluctant to buy smaller, more energy-efficient automobiles. Further, U.S. industry has installed energy-efficient capital equipment more slowly than might otherwise have been the case. Producers, concerned about the vagaries of government regulatory policy, have been reluctant to initiate projects to develop alternative energy sources.

Each oil-importing government should review its domestic energy-pricing policies and take steps necessary to move its domestic prices as rapidly as possible to world market levels. For the United States, one way to accomplish this would be to eliminate current price controls by deregulating the price of new natural gas at the wellhead and by gradually removing price controls on crude oil and petroleum products.

However, even if prices are moved up to world market levels, the response in the industrialized world may not be adequate to prevent a shortage of the type described earlier. World oil prices today are well below the cost of producing such easily substitutable alternative sources as liquefied and gasified coal, oil from shale, et cetera and are likely to remain at these levels as new Saudi, Iraqi, Alaskan, North Sea, and Mexican production comes onto the market, satisfying expected demand growth and offsetting production declines from existing fields for the next five to ten years.

If prices remain at or near current levels, there will be little incentive to develop readily substitutable alternative sources or to reduce demand growth as rapidly as would be desirable, given the pessimistic forecast for the late 1980s. Thus, even with removal of current artificial price constraints, the prospective oil "crunch" could nevertheless trigger sudden, steep increases in energy costs at some future date. As several experts have pointed out, it is not price increases *per se*, but rapid and unexpected price increases that are especially damaging to economic growth and stability.

What is needed, then, is an anticipation of and gradual approach to an era of higher petroleum prices. The advantages of such an approach would include clearer incentives for the immediate development of alternative sources of energy and a more rapid reduction in the rate of demand growth. For these reasons, it may be appropriate to consider various mechanisms for increasing prices gradually over the next several years.

Impose Specific Energy Taxes

One possible means of achieving these gradual price increases would be agreement on specific energy taxes which individual countries might impose on those sectors of their economies where significant savings are possible; an obvious example is a higher federal excise tax on gasoline in the United States. Another means is suggested by the crude oil tax proposed by the Japanese government. Such taxes could provide the revenues needed to finance subsidies for pilot or demonstration plant projects to test new energy technologies or to improve public transportation systems.

Certainly, there are many difficulties associated with an attempt to increase prices in industrialized nations above world market levels in a coordinated manner. A key danger is that producers would view the imposition of additional taxes as an excuse to raise prices and attempt to capture the possible revenue increases for themselves.

In a purely analytical sense, too, calculating and achieving consensus regarding hypothetical long-term energy replacement costs—presumably the final price level in the hypothetical "bridge"—would pose a formidable obstacle. Yet, despite these difficulties, if we take seriously the idea of an orderly, phased, and equitable transition to a new, more expensive mix of energy sources, we must recognize that price signals have to play a central role in assuring that transition. Neither consumers nor investors are going to alter their behavior on the basis of exhortation alone.

ENERGY PRODUCTION IN THE NONOIL PRODUCING LDCs

Many of the nonoil producing LDCs have large reserves of liquid and solid hydrocarbons, as well as untapped hydroelectric power sites. In addition, many of these countries have the potential to make extensive use of solar energy and other "soft" technologies.[9] To the extent that these countries develop their indigenous resources, they ease the competition for OPEC supplies, stimulate internal economic growth, and strengthen their financial position vis-à-vis the rest of the world. To the extent that they become committed to "soft energy paths," they become less dependent on nuclear generating facilities, and thus lessen the risk of nuclear proliferation. It would seem, therefore, clearly in the interest of the major industrialized oil importers to encourage development of LDC indigenous coal, oil, and gas production as well as "soft path" technology.

One constraint on such development is that the international energy companies, faced with rising threats of expropriation, are becoming reluctant to provide the necessary technology and capital. When such investments are successful, they are often expropriated or taken over by governments at less than an adequate return; of course, when they are not successful, there is no return on investment. However, mechanisms might be developed to ensure that LDCs receive the technical assistance and financing necessary to exploit their indigenous energy resources; one avenue for such assistance might be through the World Bank. The Bank already has instituted programs to provide private companies with appropriate financial guarantees and to assure technical support for LDCs.

In addition, the United States has begun a small program of non-nuclear aid to LDCs. These programs should be expanded, and other industrialized countries should be encouraged to provide similar support. As a first step in broadening efforts to develop indigenous LDC energy resources, the IEA or some other international organization should be charged with assessing LDC resources and the prospects for future LDC production as well as requirements for technical assistance and financing.

OIL IMPORT REDUCTION TARGETS

The Governing Board of the IEA in October, 1977, adopted a communique which, in addition to listing a number of broad principles upon which members had agreed as a guide to energy policies, endorsed the objective of holding total 1985 IEA imports to a level of no more than 26 million barrels per day. This decision followed a detailed review, coordinated by the IEA Secretariat, of individual country activities in energy. As a group target, 26 million barrels a day is a good beginning; but it is also true, unfortunately, that a broad "group" target of this kind, or even regional targets, provides little concrete basis for assessing national performance. The major oil-importing nations should establish specific individual targets both for reduction in the growth of demand and for increased production.

Reduction in the Growth of Demand

A major step which can be taken to delay (or perhaps even eliminate) the risk of an unacceptably large price increase is to reduce the rate of energy demand growth and thereby postpone a "supply crunch." To achieve meaningful improvements in energy efficiency, the historic linkage between economic growth and energy demand growth must be broken—through increases in the real costs of energy, through more careful planning, and through greater public appreciation of energy-saving methods and techniques.

Among the major oil-importing countries, the United States is the only one which, by its policy decisions alone, can significantly alter the prospects for a near-term demand-supply imbalance. In this important sense, other oil importers must look to American leadership for the most important step in averting a serious energy problem.[10]

While demand for energy in the U.S. was dampened by the post-1973 recession, economic recovery and an unusually cold winter had driven total energy consumption in 1976 up some 4.8 percent above the preceding year. This sharp upturn suggests that the historical pattern of annual increases in energy use (increments in excess of 4 percent) has remained unchanged or, at best, has been reduced only slightly. The lack of any careful analysis of the relationship of economic growth and energy consumption makes it difficult to know whether this relationship has, in fact, changed as the result of higher prices and the mandatory conservation programs put into place since 1973. However the evidence to date is not encouraging.

Because of the size of the U.S. economy and its overall importance in world energy consumption, obviously there is a special need for decisive U.S. action. The U.S. has a relatively high level of per capita consumption of energy; although France, Germany, England, Italy, and Japan are all using significantly less oil per unit of production than they did in 1973, the U.S. is using virtually the same amount.

There are immediate steps which can be taken in the United States to reduce demand growth and convert existing oil-fired facilities to coal. Even these steps will not have a large short-term impact on U.S. consumption, but—if decisive moves are made—they will signal that the United States is at last moving to curb oil imports. Lack of firm U.S. action will, on the other hand, send a signal of continued drift.

Increased Production

Many of the major oil-importing countries have opportunities to expand indigenous energy supplies over the next decade, and by doing so, to reduce the need for imports. Yet, environmental and resource constraints place certain limits on such expansion.

Again, as in the case of demand reduction, the commitment and leadership of the U.S., with its important offshore oil and gas potential and its vast coal reserves, will be critical. It will also be important, however, for North Sea oil producers to cooperate in this effort and for there to be agreement on goals for expanding coal and nuclear electrical generating facilities.

With respect to coal, the U.S. should take the initiative in developing an international agreement to assure European countries and Japan that they can have access to U.S. coal exports on acceptable terms. With respect to nuclear power, it is especially important to revise estimates of generating capacity carefully so that these reflect realistic assessments of future requirements and capabilities. However, the prospects for increases in nuclear power generation involve unique policy considerations that will be discussed subsequently.

The industrialized oil-importing countries should set specific production-increase targets for each major energy source to complement targets for reduced demand. International mechanisms should be improved for monitoring, analyzing, and reporting on the performance of such countries in meeting these targets. The resulting studies and assessments should be published and widely circulated, not restricted to official use as several IEA reviews have been in the past. Unless such an arrangement can be agreed upon, it will continue to be difficult both to hold countries accountable for energy policy actions and to plan intelligently for the energy situation we will face in the mid-1980s and thereafter.

NUCLEAR POLICY

It is of the utmost importance that agreement be reached as quickly as possible on a strategy for the development of nuclear power. Although it is clear that nuclear power will continue to play a part in the future energy systems of many countries, and that the further development of this energy source can reduce dependence upon imported oil, many important questions remain to be resolved with respect to the nuclear option. The recent U.S. nuclear initiatives—designed to reduce the motivation as well as the technical ability of nations to acquire nuclear weapons—have caused deep concern in other countries. The concern is that any limitation on the development of either the spent fuel reprocessing facilities or of the breeder reactor will increase the already heavy dependence of the industrialized world on OPEC oil.

The United States has proposed an International Nuclear Fuel Cycle Evaluation (INFCE) to consider these issues, and initial meetings have taken place. This effort should result in valuable technical information for decision-making, but it is important that it be carried out in a timely manner within the three years currently scheduled and that it result in an agreement on international nuclear policy.

Among the issues that should be addressed during the course of the INFCE are the following:

1. How should the findings of the INFCE study be treated—particularly regarding institutional arrangements for reducing proliferation risks?

2. What position, if any, should be taken in response to the growing public opposition to nuclear power in a number of countries and the implications of this trend in regard to OECD and other forecasts which assume substantial nuclear power generation by the early 1980s?[11]

3. Do the problems of mounting costs, uranium supply, enrichment capacity, spent fuel disposal, and weapons proliferation change the outlook for nuclear energy?

4. Should we consider pressing for an agreement to establish regional international reprocessing centers for spent fuel? How could such centers avoid discriminating against certain countries, and what incentives would be necessary to induce countries to utilize them?

5. What should be the response to the Carter administration's call for the creation of an international fuel bank and to the suggestion that the U.S. might serve as a waste storage depository?

6. In view of the recent report by the International Atomic Energy Agency (IAEA) that the inspection system responsible for safeguarding against the diversion of peaceful nuclear material needs strengthening to improve controls and close loopholes, should the IAEA membership take a firm stand in support of immediate upgrading of this system?

7. In view of the mounting evidence of the inappropriateness of nuclear technology for many developing nations, should the industrialized nations continue to subsidize, through favorable loan terms, the purchase of nuclear exports to these areas—especially when funds might thereby be directed away from the "softer" technologies?

RESEARCH AND DEVELOPMENT

In order to prepare for the eventual decline in availability of world oil supplies and to develop new, reliable, environmentally safe and renewable sources of energy, a substantial increase in commitments of funds and attention to research and development is necessary.

This need is especially urgent, given the problem of the long lead times involved both in developing new technologies and in securing significant production from them.

Each of the industrialized oil-importing countries should assess its own R & D needs and focus its efforts on the areas that offer the most significant potential payoff, areas, for example, in which it is particularly vulnerable or has unique advantages for development. The United States has great opportunities in regard to improved energy efficiency and increased use of its vast coal reserves; consequently much of its R&D activity might be directed toward conservation and coal conversion. Other countries, like Japan, might seek more balanced R&D programs, where, for example, a heavily nuclear-oriented program might be broadened to provide increased attention to solar and other alternative energy sources.

In addition to the contributions of national R&D activity, the goal of developing new sources could profit enormously from bilateral and multilateral international efforts.

For example, it appears that there may be support in both the United States and Japan for the creation of joint research programs on solar energy and nuclear fusion. In any such program, the door should be left open for participation by other countries and results should be widely disseminated.

IMPORT ALLOCATION CONTINGENCY PLAN

Finally, should all other strategies fail and we be faced in ten to fifteen years with a "worst case" situation in which supply shortages and price increases threaten to have unacceptable economic and political consequences, the major oil-importing nations must have a "last resort" contingency plan. They should begin to develop the conceptual framework and the broad specifications of an import-sharing system—

not one designed as a response to an embargo, such as the present IEA system, but one designed to contain competition for scarce oil supplies among the advanced industrial countries.

If the broad principles for establishing such a system were negotiated in advance, governments would be in a better position to put it into place in the event that OPEC production limits are reached and shortages (and sharp price increases) begin to develop. The Brussels Agreement of 1975 on emergency oil sharing provides a helpful precedent. However, realistic planning for authoritative, continuing sharing of available imports requires a degree of consensus and institutional cooperation extending far beyond that which has been possible to date.

Yet, the world's energy future remains so unclear, and—in the worst case—the possibility exists of a serious shortage in which the wealthier countries would bid up the price of available oil and deny adequate access to the LDCs and perhaps to each other as well. It is not too soon, therefore, to begin thinking about the specifications of a system which would remain "on the shelf" but be available in the event of a crisis. At the very least, a proposal to begin a study of such a system should be on the agenda of any forthcoming international energy conferences which might take place. Any decision to study the possibility of such an import sharing system, of course, should be presented in such a way as to invite broad cooperation by many countries.

NEED FOR BETTER PUBLIC UNDERSTANDING AND IMPROVED ENERGY INFORMATION

Successful adoption and implementation of these strategies by the industrialized oil-importing democracies will require broad public support. That support, in turn, depends upon public understanding of the nature and seriousness of the problem. No significant advance measures will be possible unless the average citizen in these countries recognizes the threat that the "worst case" energy scenario poses to his security and welfare and to the security and welfare of the citizens of allied nations. Although "energy crisis" has become a household expression during the past four years, public understanding of the "crisis" remains inadequate, especially in the United States. Leaders in the industrialized world must forcefully and continuously address this problem.

A contribution to better public understanding could be made by improving the quality, reliability, and dissemination of information on the energy situation. Elsewhere, the need has been cited for improved collection of data (for example, on progress made to meet oil import targets); broadened IEA audits of member countries and other periodic collection of data on energy developments should be given the widest possible distribution and visibility.

CONCLUSIONS

This outline of strategies for the future is not intended to suggest either a comprehensive or an unchanging response to the energy situation. If the experience of recent years has imparted any wisdom, it is that the breadth and complexity of world energy problems defy comprehensive or inflexible proposals for solution.

Rather, these strategies are intended to highlight areas that, obviously, require attention and to indicate the directions in which we must move *in view of* the prospective supply-demand problem which the OECD and CIA studies forecast for the late 1980s or early 1990s. The economic implications of that problem—as well as its social and political implications—dwarf the difficulties that we have thus far encountered.

In outlining these strategies, an effort has been made to underscore several key factors which should strongly influence development of energy policy. First, the energy problem is international in nature. Although certain countries—the United States and Saudi Arabia, for example—may have greater impact on its resolution than others, there is no such thing as a U.S. "energy crisis" or a European "energy crisis." There *is* a worldwide energy problem which could produce a worldwide crisis affecting every nation on earth. Secondly, solutions to the energy problem will involve long lead times—lead times associated with both increased energy production and improved energy efficiency, and involving both conventional and new resources and technologies. This consideration in turn suggests a final factor, or characteristic, of the energy problem: the problem will, for the immediate future, be relatively invisible. If and when it arises with a supply-demand "crunch," it will do so very suddenly. In this regard, it is worth noting that four years after the oil embargo energy policies in the United States and other industrialized oil-importing nations remain, for the most part, embryonic. If we fail to anticipate and prepare for the far greater implications of the coming era of high-priced energy and, as a result, permit it to arrive suddenly ten or fifteen years hence, we will be denied the luxury of such indecisiveness.

At the outset of this chapter, it was noted that the role of energy in future economic developments could well involve not just economic growth versus stagnation but economic growth versus collapse. The most recent studies, indicate that the prospects for such dire consequences are very real indeed—unless actions, like those proposed earlier, are taken and taken soon. Thus, although the developments in energy have created short-term economic problems, rising energy prices in the future need not lead to long-term stagnation or collapse. Rising prices, in fact, are perfectly compatible with long-term stability and growth in the U.S. and world economies. This more desirable scenario, however, depends upon a careful fashioning of energy's role in the years immediately ahead—a fashioning that permits prices to rise gradually and avoids the kind of sudden and sharp increase associated with a "supply crunch" which could spell economic collapse.

NOTES

1. *World Energy Outlook* (Paris: Organization for Economic Co-operation and Development, 1977); *The International Energy Situation: Outlook to 1985* (Washington, D.C.: U.S. Central Intelligence Agency, 1977); *Energy: Global Prospects 1985-2000*, Workshop on Alternative Energy Strategies (Cambridge, Mass.: Massachusetts Institute of Technology, 1977).

2. OPEC production capacity is defined as the maximum sustainable production for ninety days without regard to government restriction. Usable oil-producing capacity, which takes into account officially imposed ceilings on crude production in Saudi Arabia (8.5 million barrels per day), Kuwait (2 million barrels per day), Abu

Dhabi (1.35 million barrels per day), and Venezuela (2.3 million barrels per day), is estimated to be approximately 32.7 million barrels per day or only 1.3 million barrels per day more than required OPEC production in 1978.

3. The specific year in which shortages occur depends upon assumptions about economic growth, energy price, the strength of government policies in pursuing alternative strategies, OPEC production limits, et cetera.

4. The Conservation Commission of the World Energy Conference (London) is currently preparing still another forecast study. A preliminary report, entitled "World Energy Demand, 1985-2020," was presented to the Conference at its 10th annual meeting in Istanbul in September 1977. The conclusions of the World Energy Conference Study as summarized in this preliminary report are entirely compatible with the WAES study reviewed here: "World demand for oil will increase until the period 1985 to 1995 when consumption will become constrained within the limits set by potential oil supply." (p.1)

5. *Energy: Global Prospects 1985-2000,* Chapter 3.

6. *Higher Oil Prices and the World Economy: The Adjustment Problem,* (Washington, D.C.: Brookings Institution, 1975).

7. *Ibid.*

8. While approximately half of U.S. energy needs are satisfied with oil and half of that oil is imported, the degree of dependence of other oil importers is much greater. In West Germany and Japan, for example, oil accounts for about 50 and 70 percent of energy consumption, respectively, yet virtually all of that oil is imported. Thus, almost half of Germany's energy supply and almost three-fourths of Japan's energy supply could be placed in jeopardy by import disruptions.

9. Such technologies may be of greater relative value to LDCs than to industralized nations which have highly developed energy infrastructures. For example, "soft" technology electricity generation would tend to be more decentralized than that found in heavily industrialized countries and, consequently, could be employed without the additional burden of creating elaborate grid systems for delivery of power to consumers.

10. Japan, of course, also expects to have a significant increase in oil imports in the 1977-1985 period. Yet, it is probably true that Japan—which consumes less than one-third as much energy per capita as the U.S.—does not have the same capacity for reducing energy demand growth.

11. It is instructive to review the comments in the OECD report on this subject. "If OECD governments were to decide to shift away from nuclear power as the primary future means of generating electricity on safety and environmental grounds, the consequences for increased oil imports could be grave." *World Energy Outlook.*

SIX

The Service Industries

and U.S. Economic Growth

Since World War II

Victor R. Fuchs

Vice-President, National Bureau of Economic Research
and
Professor of Economics, Stanford University

"The most important concomitant of economic progress," wrote Colin Clark in 1940, is "the movement of labor from agriculture to manufacture, and from manufacture to commerce and services."[1] Subsequent developments have been fully consistent with Clark's observation, and this close relationship between economic growth and the expansion of service employment has been discussed by many economists.[2]

Until after World War II, the increase in the service sector's share of total U.S. employment was largely at the "expense" of agriculture; employment in industry was also expanding rapidly. Since then, service employment has continued to expand rapidly with both industry and agriculture experiencing large decreases in relative shares. In a series of studies conducted in the 1960s, I concluded that the primary reason for the shift of employment from industry to service was the more rapid rate of growth of productivity in industry.[3]

The sector difference in productivity advance has aroused fears that the shift to services will slow down growth for the economy as a whole.

Does a "service economy" imply a "stagnant economy"? This chapter first examines recent trends (the past 15 years) in employment, output, and productivity to determine whether the sector differentials have persisted. These trends and their impact on the overall growth of the economy are analyzed. The relationship between the service sector and the growth of female and government employment is considered, the projections of population, employment, and output through the end of this century are presented. The paper concludes with a few speculative observations concerning services and growth.

DEFINITIONS

The comparison of sector trends necessarily involves some arbitrary definitions. My definition of the service sector includes wholesale and retail trade, finance, insurance and real estate, general government, and professional, personal, business, and repair services. This sector is compared with industry (including mining, construction, manufacturing, transportation, communications and public utilities, and government enterprise) and agriculture. Some comparisons will also be made with agriculture and government eliminated (i.e., the private non-agriculture economy).

The time period analyzed is from 1961 to 1976. The choice of initial and terminal years is important because the *relative* importance of services tends to rise in slack periods and decline in boom years. It was desirable to extend the analysis as close to the present as possible (i.e., 1976), and 1961 is a year of comparable slackness, although it was the trough of a recession while 1976 was not. The overall unemployment rates were 6.7 percent in 1961 and 7.7 percent in 1976. Probably more relevant are the unemployment rates for males twenty years of age and over which were 5.7 percent in 1961 and 5.9 percent in 1976.

As a check on the sensitivity to choice of years, the trends between two prosperous years, 1956 and 1973, also were calculated. The results were very similar. Employment growth between 1956 and 1973 was somewhat slower than in 1961-76 for each sector, but the industry-service trend differential varied by less than 0.1 percent per annum. The 1961-76 period is compared with earlier post-World War II trends measured from 1948 to 1965, two years with identical unemployment rates for adult males.

It should be noted that significant revisions of the national income accounts were undertaken in recent years.[4] These revisions affected sector levels and also had some effect on rates of change. For this reason the changes from 1948 to 1965 were recalculated, although the results are sufficiently close to those I reported in *The Service Economy* to permit reliance on the analyses presented there.

EMPLOYMENT

Table 6.1 shows that the differential in growth trends in employment which characterized the first two decades following World War II have continued in recent years. The industry-service differential was 1.69 percentage points in the earlier period (2.18 and .49) compared with 1.34 percentage points per annum from 1961 to 1976 (2.48 and 1.14), but this difference was attributable entirely to a relative decline in the armed forces between 1961 and 1976. The industry-service differential, excluding the armed forces, was about 1.6 percentage points per annum in both periods. Agriculture continued to lose ground relatively and absolutely, but because it has become such a small part of the economy, the expansion of the service sector has been more at the expense of industry than was true in earlier periods. Thus, even the industry-service comparison omitting government shows a large differential trend.

The decline in industry's *share* is manifest in all the major groups, including manufacturing, which grew at only one percent per annum. The increase in the service sector's share was led by the services proper with a growth of 3.1 percent per annum. Some authors like to stress *intra*-sector variability (and it exists), but it is instructive to note that the slowest growing part of the service sector, retail trade, grew more rapidly than construction, the fastest growing major group in industry.

GROSS DOMESTIC PRODUCT AND SECTOR PRODUCTIVITY

The continued shift to the service sector is also evident in gross domestic product measured in current dollars as shown in Table 6.2.

Table 6.1   Levels and Rates of Change of Employment[a] by Sector, Selected Years, 1948-76

Part A: Sector shares (percent)

	1948	1961	1965	1976
Total economy				
Agriculture	10.8	6.9	5.5	4.2
Industry	43.2	38.6	39.1	35.1
Service	46.0	54.5	55.4	60.7
Private[b] nonagriculture				
Industry	54.0	48.4	48.6	43.0
Service	46.0	51.6	51.4	57.0

Part B: Rates of change (percent per annum)[c]

	1948-65	1961-76
Total economy	1.08	1.76
Agriculture	−2.91	−1.63
Industry	.49	1.14
Service	2.18	2.48
(excluding armed forces)	(2.08)	(2.70)
Private[b] nonagriculture		
Industry	.42	1.09
Service	1.71	2.56

SOURCES: *The National Income and Product Accounts of the United States, 1947-1974, Statistical Tables* for 1948, 1961 and 1965 (Washington, D.C.: U.S. Office of Business Economics); and *Survey of Current Business,* July 1977 (for 1976).

[a]Full-time equivalent persons engaged.
[b]Excludes government.
[c]Continuously compounded.

Indeed, by this criterion the shift from industry to service accelerated slightly in the 1961-76 period. When output is measured in constant (1972) dollars as in Table 6.3, however, very little shift from industry to service is observed. Apart from the decline of agriculture there has been very little change in sector shares of gross product in constant dollars for half a century!

The sector trends in productivity, presented in Table 6.4, are

Table 6.2 Levels and Rates of Change of Gross Domestic Product in Current Dollars by Sector, Selected Years 1948-76

Part A: Sector shares (percent)

	1948	1961	1965	1976
Total economy				
Agriculture	9.3	4.2	3.5	3.1
Industry	46.8	45.0	45.6	41.2
Service	43.9	50.8	50.9	55.7
Private nonagriculture				
Industry	55.1	51.6	52.0	47.2
Service	44.9	48.4	48.0	52.8

Part B: Rates of change (percent per annum)

	1948-65	1961-76
Total economy	5.70	7.86
Agriculture	− .05	5.98
Industry	5.55	7.26
Service	6.56	8.48
Private nonagriculture		
Industry	5.51	7.19
Service	6.26	8.37

SOURCES AND NOTES: See Table 6.1.

derived in the following way: The actual rate of output per worker is simply the rate for gross domestic product in constant (1972) dollars minus the rate of growth of employment. The rates relative to the total economy for output per unit of labor input (and output per unit of total factor input) are derived by assuming that factor prices change at the same rate in all sectors. If so, the sector change in total labor compensation (or total compensation to all factors) relative to the change for all sectors is approximately equal to the change in labor input (or total factor input) in that sector relative to that for the economy as a whole.[5]

The industry-service differential in growth of output per worker was lower in 1961-76 than in 1948-65, but the sector differences in the two other productivity measures were somewhat larger in the more re-

Table 6.3   Levels and Rates of Change of Gross Domestic Product in Constant (1972) Dollars, by Sector, Selected Years 1948-76

Part A: Sector shares (percent)

	1948	1961	1965	1976
Total economy				
Agriculture	5.8	4.3	3.6	2.9
Industry	43.0	40.7	43.2	40.7
Service	51.3	55.0	53.2	56.3
Private nonagriculture				
Industry	50.8	48.2	50.3	46.7
Service	49.2	51.8	49.7	53.3

Part B: Rates of change (percent per annum)

	1948-65	1961-76
Total economy	3.74	3.51
Agriculture	.97	.87
Industry	3.77	3.52
Service	3.96	3.67
Private nonagriculture		
Industry	3.86	3.56
Service	3.98	3.97

SOURCES AND NOTES: See Table 6.1.

cent period. For 1948-65 almost half of the sector differences in growth of output per person was attributable to differential changes in hours of work, quality of labor, and capital per worker.[6] These differences were apparently much less important in recent years.

OVERALL PRODUCTIVITY

One of the most striking features of Table 6.4 is the general retardation in the growth of output per worker in 1961-76 compared with 1948-65. It is this slowdown in overall productivity advance which some observers seek to attribute to the growth of services. A few simple

Table 6.4 Rates of Change of Productivity by Sector, 1948-65 and 1961-76 (percent per annum)

	1948-65	1961-76
Actual rates		
Output per worker		
Total economy	2.66	1.75
Agriculture	3.88	2.50
Industry	3.28	2.38
Service	1.78	1.19
Service, excluding government	2.27	1.41
Rates relative to the total economy		
Output per unit of labor input		
Agriculture	+2.05	−.37
Industry	+.41	+.67
Service	−.60	−.49
Service, excluding government	−.04	−.07
Output per unit of total factor input		
Agriculture	+2.98	−.76
Industry	+.18	+.61
Service	−.64	−.46
Service, excluding government	−.32	−.05

SOURCE: Tables 6.1, 6.2, and 6.3.

calculations, however, show that sector shifts can explain only a very small part of the slowdown.

When output shares remain constant over time an index of aggregate output per worker is simply a weighted average of the indexes of output per worker in each sector where the weights are terminal year employment shares.[7] If one applies the 1965 sector distribution of employment to the 1961-76 sector trends in productivity, or if one applies the 1976 sector distribution to the 1948-65 sector trends, the alteration in the rate of growth of output per worker for the total economy is only .1 percent per annum compared with the rates actually observed. Even these calculations overstate the effect of the shift from industry to service because part of the .1 percent per annum sector distribution effect is attributable to the decline of agriculture, not shifts within the nonagriculture sector.

This should not come as a surprise. Grossman and I simulated productivity trends for fifty years into the future under a wide variety of assumptions about sector shares of output and employment, as well as trends in these shares. We found that the shift to services would have only a small effect on national productivity growth.[8] Moreover, Table 6.4 shows clearly that the slowdown in productivity growth was present *in each sector.* It was largest in agriculture and smallest in service, with a decline in industry slightly larger than the decline for the total economy.

It is not our purpose at this time to discuss the deceleration in productivity growth in all its aspects, but a few comments seem warranted. First, it is important to note that real output grew almost as rapidly in 1961-76 as in 1948-65 (see Table 6.3). Looked at purely in statistical terms, the slowdown in productivity growth was accounted for primarily by the *acceleration* in the growth of employment from 1.1 percent to 1.8 percent per annum as illustrated in Table 6.1.

Second, it should be noted that *output per capita,* as distinct from *output per worker,* grew more rapidly in 1961-76 than in 1948-65; see Table 6.5. The acceleration in employment growth was not due to a faster growth of population in general (population growth actually slowed down), but to a sharp increase in the population of working age. It is true that employment grew somewhat more rapidly than did the working age population in 1961-76 (because of the rise in female labor force participation), but this was also true in 1948-65.

FEMALE EMPLOYMENT

It might be thought that the rapid increase in female employment was a significant reason for the acceleration of total employment in recent years, but Table 6.5 shows that this was not true. Both male and female employment accelerated. The fact that female employment grew more rapidly than male in both periods and that females' share of employment was larger in the second period contributed only .1 percent per annum to the change in overall employment growth.

The extremely rapid growth of female employment explains a sig-

Table 6.5   Rates of Change of Output, Population, and Employment, 1948-65 and 1961-76 (percent per annum)

	1948-65	1961-76
Output[a]	3.74	3.51
Population[b]	1.66	1.05
Output per capita	2.08	2.46
Population 20-64 years of age[b]	.86	1.45
Population under 20 and 65 or over[b]	2.63	.60
Employment (f-t-e)[c]	1.08	1.76
Employment (civilian full-time and part-time)[b]	1.16	1.90
Male[b]	.62	1.22
Female[b]	2.34	3.09

SOURCES: [a]Table 6.3
[b]*Economic Report of the President, January 1977* (Washington, D.C.: Council of Economic Advisers, January, 1977).
[c]Full-time equivalent. Table 6.1.

nificant portion of total employment growth since 1948. Of the 30 million workers added to the U.S. labor force between 1948 and 1976, almost 20 million were women. The growth of female employment does *not*, however, explain the acceleration of total employment in 1961-76 because the sex differential was present in both periods.

Female labor force participation has been studied by many economists in recent years,[9] but a full explanation of the dramatic rise of recent decades has not yet been provided. Much of the research emphasizes the general rise in wage rates (for men and women) or shifts in the supply curve of female labor. I believe this is part of the story, but I believe another important and frequently neglected part is the particularly rapid growth in *demand for female labor* due to the expansion of the service sector. Of particular importance is the location of many service industries in residential areas and the greater flexibility in hours of work.

With the aid of Census of Population data on employment by sex and industry group, we can make a rough estimate of how much the expansion of the service industries contributed to the growth of female employment. In Table 6.6 the growth rates for females and males and the differential between them are decomposed into the portion at-

Table 6.6   Rates of Growth of Female and Male Employment, 1950 to 1970 (percent per annum)

	Female	Male	Female minus male
(1) Actual	3.26	.94	2.32
Attributable to:			
(2) Change in industry mix[a]	.69	−.33	1.02
(3) Change in female's share[b]	.88	−.42	1.30
(4) Change in total economy[c]	1.69	1.69	0

SOURCE: U.S. Bureau of the Census, *Censuses of Population, 1950 and 1970,* Summary Volumes.

[a]Assumes constant female share and constant total.
[b]Assumes constant industry mix and constant total.
[c]Assumes constant female share and constant industry mix.

Table 6.7   Changes in Male and Female Employment between 1950 and 1970

	Employment 1950 1970 (thousands)		Change in employment, 1950-70		Relative gain or loss in employment[a] (thousands)
	1950	1970	Absolute (thousands)	Rate (% per annum)	
Total	54,275	76,149	21,874	1.69	0
Male	39,364	47,505	8,141	.94	−7,724
Female	14,911	28,644	13,733	3.26	+7,724
Female: prof. & rel. svcs.	2,707	8,527	5,820	5.74	+4,729
Female: other svc. sector	7,501	12,779	5,278	2.66	+2,255
Female: excl. svc. sector	4,703	7,338	2,635	2.22	+740
Male: prof. & rel. svcs.	1,952	4,950	2,998	4.65	+2,210
Male: other svc. sector	12,745	16,980	4,235	1.43	−902
Male: excl. svc. sector	24,666	25,575	909	.18	−9,032

SOURCE: U.S. Bureau of the Census, *Censuses of Population, 1950 and 1970,* Summary Volumes.

[a]Difference between actual change (column 3) and change if sector had grown at the national rate for all sectors.

tributable to changes in industry mix and the portion attributable to increase in the female share of employment within each industry. We see that the change in mix (at the one-digit level) contributed almost one-half of the total sex differential in employment growth.

Table 6.7 shows the relation between the expansion of services and the growth of female employment in a particularly striking way. The *relative* gain in female employment between 1950 and 1970 (the extent to which female employment in 1970 was larger than what it would have been if it had grown at the national rate) was 7.7 million jobs. Of this number, 4.7 million were obtained in professional and related services, 2.3 million in other services industries, and only .7 million in the rest of the economy. To be sure, the complex relationship between sector and sex differentials in employment growth is not captured in such a simple calculation. The growth in demand for services may be partly a *result* of an increase in female labor force participation rather than a cause, but Tables 6.6 and 6.7 do, it seems to me, reveal an important part of the total story.

GOVERNMENT EMPLOYMENT

Along with the growth of female employment, another startling feature of the post-World War II U.S. economy has been the rapid growth of government employment. By 1976 more than one in six employed persons was on a government payroll; the ratio was less than 10 percent in 1948. These data are frequently used to attack "bureaucratic proliferation." The implication is that government agencies have been multiplying and expanding in accordance with Parkinson's Law. An alternative interpretation is that there has been very little expansion of government employment in the sense of government taking over the production of goods and services that were formerly produced in the private sector. Instead, what has happened is that certain industries in the service sector (e.g., health, education) have grown particularly rapidly in recent decades, and these industries happen to be those in which government traditionally has played a significant role. According to this view, the shift from private to government employment should be seen largely as a consequence of the growth of a service economy.

Table 6.8   Rates of Growth of Government and Private Employment, 1950 to 1970 (percent per annum)

	Government (A)	Government (B)	Private (A)	Private (B)	Government minus private (A)	Government minus private (B)
(1) Actual	4.04	4.98	1.34	1.34	2.70	3.64
Attributable to:						
(2) Change in industry mix[a]	1.81	2.45	− .08	− .08	1.89	2.53
(3) Change in government's share[b]	.54	.89	− .27	− .22	.81	1.11
(4) Change in total economy[c]	1.69	1.64	1.69	1.64	0	0

SOURCE: U.S. Bureau of the Census, *Censuses of Population, 1950 and 1970,* Summary Volumes.

(A) Includes all industries.
(B) Includes all industries except postal service and public administration.
[a]Assumes constant government share and constant total.
[b]Assumes constant industry mix and constant total.
[c]Assumes constant government share and constant industry mix.

The data give considerable support to the second interpretation. Table 6.8 presents the results of a shift and share analysis of employment growth rates between 1950 and 1970 similar to that presented in Table 6.6. Using census data on employment cross-classified by industry and class of worker, I have decomposed the growth of government and private employment into the portion attributable to differential industry growth (change in industry mix), the portion attributable to shifts between the private and government sectors within each industry (government share), and the portion attributable to the growth of the total economy. This calculation is done (A) with all industries and (B) excluding postal service and public administration, which always have 100 percent in government. The results are qualitatively similar in both cases. The first row of Table 6.8 shows a substantial differential in the growth of government and private employment over the two decades amounting to 2.70 or 3.64 percent per annum, depending upon whether postal service and public administration are included or excluded. The next two rows show that most of this differential is attributable to the differential rate of growth of industries (i.e., the

Table 6.9   Changes in Private and Government Employment between 1950 and 1970

	Employment 1950 1970 (thousands)	Change in employment, 1950-1970 Absolute (thousands)	Rate (% per annum)	Relative gain or loss in employment[a] (thousands)
Total	54,275 76,149	21,874	1.69	0
Private	48,786 63,829	15,043	1.34	−4,619
Government	5,489 12,321	6,832	4.04	+4,619
Private, excl. professional and related services	46,148 56,505	10,357	1.01	−8,242
Private professional and related services	2,638 7,324	4,686	5.11	+3,623
Government professional and related services	2,021 6,152	4,131	5.57	+3,316
Postal service	454 719	265	2.30	+82
Public administration[b]	2,035 3,483	1,448	2.69	+628
Other government[c]	979 1,967	988	3.49	+593

SOURCE: U.S. Department of Commerce, Bureau of Census, *1970 Census of Population,* vol. 1, *Characteristics of the Population,* part 1 U.S. Summary, Section 2, Washington, D.C., 1973, pp. 1-806, 1-808.

[a]Difference between actual absolute change (column 3) and change if sector had grown at the national rate for all sectors.
[b]Federal, state and local.
[c]Mostly construction, transportation, communications and public utilities.

change in industry mix) and less than a third is due to an increasing government share holding industry mix constant.

Table 6.9 examines the same phenomena from a somewhat different point of view. Between 1950 and 1970 total employment in the economy increased by almost 22 million, or a rate of change of 1.69 percent per annum. Private employment grew at 1.34 percent per annum, which meant that the private sector was short 4.6 million jobs compared to what it would have had if it had grown at the same rate as for the total economy. The government sector showed an equivalent relative gain in employment. The next several rows of Table 6.9, however, put this shift in a different perspective. The private sector, *excluding professional and related services,* suffered a relative loss of 8.2 million jobs between 1950 and 1970. Where did they go? The largest relative gains were in *private* professional and related services, 3.6 million. The next largest was in government professional and related services, 3.3 million. By comparison, the gains in public administration and other government were relatively small. Thus, the so-called expansion of government employment might more accurately be characterized as an expansion of professional and related services, both private and governmental.

These calculations do not, of course, capture all aspects of the expanded role government plays in the economy. There has been a large increase in government serving as a financial intermediary for retirement benefits, medical insurance, and the like. There has also been a huge increase in regulatory intervention, especially with respect to activities and products that might affect health. But the data do not support frequently voiced simplistic charges about a "government takeover" of economic production.

SUMMARY OF FINDINGS

The principal findings to this point are:
1. During the past 15 years, employment and current dollar gross product continued to shift to the service sector at about the same rate as in the early post-World War II period.
2. The service sector's share of gross product in constant dollars remained relatively constant; productivity (as measured in the National Income Accounts) continued to grow less rapidly than in industry or agriculture.
3. The rate of growth of output per worker for the total economy was almost *one percent* per annum less than in 1948-65. This reflected a slight decrease in the rate of growth of output and a sharp acceleration in the rate of growth of employment.
4. The shift to the service sector contributed less than .1 percent per annum to the decrease in productivity growth.
5. The acceleration in employment growth is explained almost entirely by a sharp increase in the population of working age. Total population growth was much less than in 1948-65, and output *per capita* actually rose more rapidly in 1961-76.

6. Female labor force participation rates have risen at a very rapid rate throughout the post-World War II period, in part because of the expansion of the service sector. On the other hand, female employment was *not* a significant factor in either the acceleration of employment or the slowdown of productivity growth in 1961-76.

7. Government employment has grown at a very rapid rate in recent decades. The principal reason is the expansion of service industries, such as health and education, in which government has traditionally played a large role. Apart from changes in industry mix, the expansion of government employment has been quite modest.

One huge caveat must be attached to the finding concerning sector differentials in productivity. As is well known, the methods used to measure "real output" in services frequently fall far short of a desirable standard. For instance, until the recent revisions,[10] output in government was simply equated with full-time-equivalent employment. Output per worker never changed, by definition. The revised method is based on employee hours in the various civil service and wage board grades weighted by the 1972 payrolls in these grades. That is, changes in the "quality" of labor measured by changes in the mix of grades are assumed to produce proportional changes in output. Changes in capital stocks or technology continue to be ignored.

Another problem area is banking. Prior to the revisions, output in banking (and other financial intermediaries except life insurance carriers) was indexed by constant dollar deposits. This produced an apparent sharp decline in banking productivity over time as the volume of services provided per constant dollar deposits rose.[11] This approach was discarded in the last revision. Now real output in banking is assumed to be proportional to full-time-equivalent employment!

The rates of growth of output and productivity in government, banking, and many other service industries are almost surely understated in the National Income Accounts. I do not, however, believe that these biases are the principal reason for the observed industry-service differential because there are also biases that work in the opposite direction. For instance, the growth of output and productivity in retailing is probably overstated because of a failure to capture a decline in services provided by retailers per constant dollar of goods sold.[12] Furthermore, there probably are large downward biases in many indexes of industry output, especially when the goods produced are complex and undergoing rapid technological change (e.g., computers).

I also do not believe that these biases can explain the slowing down of productivity growth in recent years. This slowing down seems to be a real phenomenon, the explanation for which should rather be sought in the slowing down of growth of capital per worker and in a variety of other social and economic changes.[13]

PREDICTIONS TO 1990 AND 2000

We have seen how demographic trends can have significant effects on employment, productivity, and output per capita. It may be useful, therefore, to look ahead to 1990 and 2000 and try to project growth rates for the variables under discussion. To be sure, such an exercise should be treated with great caution. The literature is replete with examples of demographic predictions and projections which proved to be far off target. For instance, Peter Drucker, usually an acute observer of economic and social trends, in a 1955 article in *Harper's* predicted an increase in population of at least 40 percent by 1975. The actual increase was only 29 percent. He no doubt failed to anticipate the tremendous decrease in the birth rate during that period. In the same article he predicted an increase in the labor force of 20 percent. The actual increase was 41 percent! The discrepancy was probably attributable primarily to a failure to anticipate the sharp rise in female labor force participation. The projections presented in Table 6.10 should, therefore, be viewed for the most part as one possible scenario rather than as firm forecasts.

Probably the most reliable projection is for the population age 20 to 64 in 1990. This figure cannot be affected by subsequent changes in the birth rate, and death rates for that age group are already sufficiently low that even further reductions, far greater than those expected, would not alter the growth rate very much. Therefore, short of a major catastrophe (not allowed for in any of the projections), we see that the population of working age will continue to grow at a very rapid rate

Table 6.10   Projected Rates of Change of Output, Population, and Employment, 1976-90 and 1990-2000 (percent per annum)

	Actual (1961-1976)	1976-1990	1990-2000
Population, 20-64	1.45	1.3	.8
Population, <20 + 65+	.60	.5	.6
Total population	1.05	.9	.7
Employment (full & parttime)			
Male	1.22	1.0	.6
Female	3.09	2.5	1.2
Total	1.90	1.7	.9
Employment (f-t-e)	1.76	1.5	.7
Gross Domestic Product			
(1976 dollars)	3.51	3.2	2.3
Output per worker	1.75	1.7	1.6
Output per capita	2.46	2.3	1.6

SOURCE: U.S. Bureau of the Census, *Current Population Reports*, series P-25.

NOTE: Population projections are taken from the Bureau of the Census for medium estimates of cohort fertility. Employment projections are based on the author's assumption that female labor force participation rates will continue to rise rapidly until 1990, move slowly thereafter, and that unemployment rates in 1990 and 2000 will be at the 1976 level. Sector growth rates of output per worker are assumed the same as in 1961-76, and sector differentials in employment growth are also expected to continue as before.

until 1990. After that point—actually beginning in the late 1980s however, there will be a noticeable retardation in the growth of population of working age.

The projections for the population under 20 and 65 and over are much more speculative because sharp changes in the birth rate or in death rates at older ages could significantly alter trends. Using the Bureau of the Census medium projections for cohort fertility rates (approximately 2.1 births per woman) and assuming a slight improvement in life expectancy, the nonworking age population will grow at only .5 percent per annum until 1990, and at a slightly more rapid rate from 1990 to 2000.[14] These rates are consistent with the low rate recorded in the 1961-76 period.

Given the rapid growth of population age 20-64 until 1990, I expect employment to grow almost as rapidly during that period as it did in 1961-76 (assuming unemployment is approximately the same in 1990 as in 1976). This projection is higher than that of the Bureau of Labor Statistics because I expect female labor force participation to increase at a more rapid rate than does the BLS.[15] For women ages 20-64 the BLS is projecting a labor force participation rate of 61 percent in 1990 compared with a current rate of about 55 percent. My projections assume a rate of 68 percent. (The comparable male rate is now, and is expected to be, about 89 percent.) It is possible that I may be correct about female employment but still be too high for total full-time-equivalent employment because male labor force participation rates may fall more rapidly than in the past, or part-time employment may increase sharply. On the other hand, my employment projection may be too low if there is a reversal of past trends toward earlier retirement.

If I am correct that female labor force participation rates will be quite high by 1990, then employment growth for 1990 to 2000 is likely to decelerate markedly. Not only will the populaton age 20-64 grow slowly during that period, but the potential contribution to employment of further increases in female labor force participation rates will be much weaker.

The final projections concerning output and productivity are the most speculative of all and are presented primarily to provide a basis for discussion. I assume that the industry and service shares of *real output* will remain relatively unchanged as they have in the past. I further assume that *output per worker* in each sector will grow at the same rate as in 1961-76, which in the cases of industry and service are approximately the same rates as for the half century since 1929.

Under these assumptions the growth rate of *total output* 1976-1990 would be only .3 percentage points per annum less than in 1961-76, and the increase in *output per capita* would be almost equal to that of the past 15 years. The decade from 1990 to 2000, however, would show a marked slowdown in the growth of output and output per capita because of the slow growth in employment. To the extent that sector increases in productivity are faster or slower than those recorded in 1961-76, the output and productivity projections would have to be modified accordingly.

CONCLUDING COMMENTS

The sector rates of productivity growth 1961-76 are low in comparison with the exceptional rates recorded in 1948-65, but they are squarely in line with longer-term trends from 1929 to 1965. Thus the question currently receiving so much attention—"Why has the rate of productivity advance slowed?"—might more reasonably be formulated "Why did productivity grow so rapidly after World War II?"

This paper rejects the hypothesis that the shift of employment to the service sector was a major cause of changes in the rate of growth of productivity and, further, calls attention to the importance of demographic trends for economic growth, both in the past and in the decades ahead. Substantial decreases in the rates of growth of employment and output per capita during 1990-2000 seem inescapable because of population trends and because the transition of women to high rates of labor force participation will be almost over.

Although output growth will slow, there is no basis for assuming a "stagnant" economy. Productivity does advance in services, albeit at a slower pace. Greater emphasis is likely to be given to the "qualitative" dimensions of life. Real GNP (as currently measured) will be increasingly unsatisfactory as an index of long-term trends in the well-being of society, and we are likely to see more effort devoted to direct measures of health, educational attainment, and other outputs of a service economy.

NOTES

[1] Colin Clark, *The Conditions of Economic Progress* (London: Macmillan, 1940).

[2] Allan G. B. Fisher, *The Clash of Progress and Security* (London: Macmillan, 1935); George Stigler, *Trends in Employment in the Service Industries* (Princeton: Princeton University Press, for the National Bureau of Economic Research, 1956), p.47; B. M. Deakin and K. D. George, "Productivity Trends in the Service Industries, 1948-63," *London and Cambridge Economic Bulletin*, March 1965; and B. D. Haig, "An Analysis of Changes in the Distribution of Employment between the Manufacturing and Service Industries, 1960-1970." *Reveiw of Economics and Statistics*, February 1975.

3. Victor R. Fuchs, *The Service Economy* (New York: Columbia University Press, 1968); and Victor R. Fuchs, ed., *Production and Productivity in the Service Industries,* Conference on Research in Income and Wealth, vol. 34 (New York: National Bureau of Economic Research, 1969).

4. See "The National Income and Product Accounts of the United States: Revised Estimates, 1929-74," *Survey of Current Business,* vol. 56, no. 1, Part I, January 1976.

5. See Fuchs, *The Service Economy,* pp. 48-50 and 204, for the justification for and qualifications of this approach.

6. *Ibid.,* pp. 60-76.

7. See Michael Grossman and Victor R. Fuchs, "Intersectoral Shifts and Aggregate Productivity Change," *Annals of Economic and Social Measurement,* 1975, p.232. This is strictly true when there is only one factor of production.

8. *Ibid.,* and see also R. E. Kutscher, J. A. Mark, and J. R. Norsworthy, "The Productivity Slowdown and the Outlook to 1985," *Monthly Labor Review,* May 1977, p.5: " . . . the shift to services, however defined, can be viewed as only a minor source of the slowdown in the rate of productivity growth."

9. Jacob Mincer, "Labor Force Participation of Married Women," in *Aspects of Labor Economics* (Princeton: Princeton University Press, for the National Bureau of Economic Research, 1962); G. Cain, *Married Women in the Labor Force* (Chicago: University of Chicago Press, 1966); Yoram Ben-Porath, "Labor Force Participation Rates and the Supply of Labor," *Journal of Political Economy,* February 1977, pp. 27-58; and James J. Heckman and Robert J. Willis, "A Beta-Logistic Model for the Analysis of Sequential Labor Force Participation by Married Women," *Journal of Political Economy,* February 1977, pp. 27-58.

10. See note 4 above.

11. John A. Gorman, "Alternative Measures of the Real Output and Productivity of Commercial Banks," in Victor R. Fuchs, *Production and Productivity in the Service Industries.*

12. David Schwartzman, "The Growth of Sales Per Man-Hour in Retail Trade, 1929-1963," in Fuchs, *Production and Productivity in the Service Industries.*

13. National Center for Productivity and Quality of Working Life, *Annual Report to the President and Congress* (Washington, D.C.: U.S. Government Printing Office, 1976). Also see "U.S. Economic Growth from 1976 to 1986: Prospects, Problems, and Patterns," *Productivity* (Washington, D.C.: Joint Economic Committee of the Congress, October 1, 1976), vol. 1.

14. U.S. Bureau of the Census, *Current Population Reports,* series P-25.

15. H. N. Fullerton, Jr. and P. O. Flaim, "New Labor Force Projections to 1990," *Monthly Labor Review,* December 1976.